YOU'LL NEVER BE NOTHING

A Child's Struggle
to Overcome His Father's Words

I held on to one entity, the audience. They were safe.

by D'everett-White

DORRANCE
PUBLISHING CO
EST. 1920
PITTSBURGH, PENNSYLVANIA 15238

Dorrance Publishing Co
585 Alpha Drive
Pittsburgh, PA 15238
Visit our website at *www.dorrancebookstore.com*

ISBN: 978-1-4809-5094-8
eISBN: 978-1-4809-5071-9

Dedication

For my mother, Lady Maggie, you are the bridge that carried me over to a place where I could feel safe....

Preface

All of our lives have been forever altered, enhanced, molded, or nurtured through a combination of positive, negative, or lack of parental influences during our formative years. The things that were said and done have undoubtedly defined who we were to become.

This true story chronicles the painful solitary journey of a boy trying to become a man under the influence of a demon in human form: his father, our father. The man sired seventeen children with three women. The last eleven children were with our mother, a woman seventeen years younger, who lived terrified and trapped along with all his children. "Dad" selectively and cruelly tortured all of them throughout many years. He sexually abused some of us, but physically, verbally, and emotionally abused all of us until we escaped one way or the other. Sadly, some escaped through drug or alcohol abuse or through incarceration. Some left home as soon as possible, marrying in their teens and wound up in bad marriages of their own.

For us, growing up was like living parallel lives as zombies, enduring untold horror, yet finding a way to cope at home, appearing to be a normal Catholic church-going family on Sunday mornings to the outside world. We had no voice, no way, and no escape.

These pages chronicle Donn's journey and his method of escape. His torture, laid out for all to see. His God-given talent became his road to survival and sanity.

My sister, Betty L. Powers

In loving memory

Betty and I were the closest of my mother's eleven children. My mother referred to us as intelligent assholes (a joke). She said we knew too much for our own good. Betty had always been a driving force in my life. She was the one usually pushing behind the scene, telling my mother, "We need to find a way." Her influence led to my going to New York and later opening on the Sunset Strip and the deal with Peggy Rogers made business manager Dick Clark Productions.

Betty never knew what drove me until I visited her in the hospital. She was there recovering from a mild heart attack brought on by Lupus. I wanted her to read some of the pages of the memoir. We talked about my entire life for the first time, and then she knew the truth behind the sadness. She asked me to leave this writing with her; she wanted to know the details. The next day she called me and told me she would be home in a few days. She had read it over and over again. She wrote the preface and four days later, she died August 2, 2005

Authentic Manhood

Author Bill Hybel once wrote, "To a generation of men failed by their father and lost in a cloud of confusion, God says, 'Don't spend a lifetime in aimless drifting. Don't succumb to mindless misinterpretation of masculine identity, enter into a relationship with me through Jesus Christ and allow me to lead you into authentic manhood. Become my adopted sons and let me re-father you.'"

The freedom of authentic masculinity is quite amazing. It produces a "divine elasticity" in men. Finally they can lead with firmness and then submit with humility. They can challenge with a cutting edge, then encourage with enthusiasm. They can fight aggressively for just causes, then moments later, weep over suffering. These are the masterpieces God had in mind when he created man. God looks at them and says, "Very good. You are magnificent creatures and authentic males." - Judges 6: 11-24

As a survivor of abuse throughout my childhood and into middle age, I found peace,
acceptance, and love in the world of entertainment. Though the words and actions of my
father haunted me most of my life, the stage was my anchor and the audience, my family.
My story is horrifying, yet hopeful. As a performer, I have met many wonderful people,

creating priceless memories and lasting relationships with show business icons like
Ella Fitzgerald, Pearl Bailey, Totie Fields, Sammy Davis Jr., and Frank Sinatra.

YOU'LL NEVER BE NOTHING

A Child's Struggle
to Overcome His Father's Words

Chapter 1: Center Stage

I made my way to the left wing of the stage where a young lady stood and handed me a cup of tea. She whispered, "Good luck tonight," and I thanked her. It was show time. I went up the stairs, deliberately taking each step and inhaling and exhaling at every two steps. The smell of a theater filled with people is totally different from an empty theater. It is warm and floral, and the lights give it the look of a bright moonlit night. I arrived at the top of the stairs and now it was, "Good evening, Mr. Everett-White," "Have a great show," and "Can I get you something, sir?" The level of respect had changed. It was theater at its best.

I stood there listening to the audience adjusting themselves in their seats and to the introduction music before it came to my cue. I thought, *Wow, here I am again.* I felt the tea cup so warm, yet my hands were ice cold. That old feeling of nausea, and my slight fear that I would pass out, was not there. It was different this time; that fearful boy was now a man, secure in his voice and his relationship with an audience. The music swelled, signaling the introduction, "Ladies and gentleman…"

As I looked out into the audience, I realized I was standing where I had stood some twenty years earlier. It had been too long since I had sung to an audience like this, since I had taken center stage. I could see their faces, their smiles, and their mouthed well-wishes as they applauded. There was love. I was home. The stage lights, so bright and so familiar, wrapped me in a warm glow, and I took a deep breath. As the introduction to the song began to play, I heard, singularly, the piano keys and the bows as they touched the violin strings; the sound was so clear. I thought, *this is where I belong. I wasted so much time*. I began the set with "What Are You Doing the Rest of Your Life?" It was perfect. Ironically, I was singing my own wake-up call.

The audience met each song with applause and standing ovations. My conversation with the audience, although rehearsed, seemed as though I was telling a simple story off the cuff, to which they responded with laughter and comments. There are many performances you can count as good or great, but on this night, every move, every gesture was poetry.

Just a few hours earlier, we had arrived at the theater around 6:00 P.M. My wife, Domino, and the kids walked through the stage doors first and I followed. It was all so familiar, except that years ago I had always arrived solo. I smelled that steel odor of an older theater. The wood floors creaked as we walked carefully across to the stairs leading to the dressing rooms. I stopped to look toward center stage where I would be standing in a couple of hours. So superstitious, I would never stand there before the audience arrived on an opening night. We made our way to the dressing room, saying hello to everyone and laughing and joking with the stage crew. "Hey, Donn, what do you think of this?" and "What do you think of that?" Everyone was so silly and light. It was a good group of people.

In the dressing room, we laughed about it being a long time coming and joked, *Was I ready for this?* But we all knew I was.

I had prepared for this and every performance the same way. I awoke that morning at five o'clock and began my normal regimen, a two- and-a-half mile walk, three-hundred crunches, three-hundred push-ups, one-hundred pull-ups in sets of twenty-five, four sets of squats, four sets of dead-lifts, stretching, and two hours of vocalizing. A light meal early in the day and protein meal late afternoon prior to performance. It was mid-summer, and Los Angeles was beautiful, very little smog and a slight breeze. That night I would come full-circle, standing on a stage at the Wiltern Theater.

That night as we drove home, I basked in performance after-glow with my wife beside me and four sleeping children in the backseat. I reflected on the turning point. It was not a moment in which things suddenly changed for the better nor was it a moment of epiphany, really. My marriage was still failing; we were still broke and broken. I was still suffering from nightmares and depression. I had no idea how I might find my way back to the stage, my place of warmth and acceptance. But the turning point initiated the process of purging a lifetime of fear and anger that had begun when I was a boy and spilled over into my life as a family man.

Times had been tough for the family financially. Our home was in foreclosure. One night months before the Wiltern performance, I put the family to bed, went downstairs, and turned on the TV. My thoughts were all over the place, but eventually landed on my childhood.

There were seventeen of us, ten boys and seven girls in our immediate family. I could not remember ever doing anything together. I was always alone. Until that night, I'd remembered only three events clearly: the assassination of John F. Kennedy, The Los Angeles Watts riots, and "The Art Linkletter Show." I was one of the kids on the show. It opened my eyes to people who were different in color. People my father said hated me because of my color.

My father and I stopped speaking after the last whipping; by the time I was old enough to understand his life, he was already dead. I was happy he was gone and sad that there was no opportunity for him ever to say he loved me. Maybe when he was growing up, the prejudices and lack of respect toward people of color in the south took away something he needed to help him love his family. Maybe he had hopes and dreams and knew he'd never be able to fulfill them.

I never felt protected at home except by my mother's love when she took a stand against the man she also feared. She was a lady in every sense of the word. She was the bridge that carried me over to a world that protected me. She always made sure I got to an audition or performance. She did her best, and I will always recognize her struggle to keep the family together when so many others would have left. The stage and the audience became my protection. I always felt secure there. People showed me love with looks of approval and applause. They opened their arms and accepted me without any question. The stage lights were warm and protecting. The people I met in show business were special, not because they were stars because I did not know of them, but because they always wished me the best. Sammy, Totie, and Ella always ended a conversation with "Wishing you the best." I miss them.

In my living room that night, with thoughts of my parents and my own parenting, I began to watch *Biography*. Would my life look better or make more sense if I were watching it as a biography instead of living it? Would it turn out to have a happy ending? I'd just attended a men's ministry workshop for chemical dependency. Willie Flores, a minister visiting Los Angeles from the New York Church of Christ, had led the discussion. He spoke about how they would focus the participants by having them keep a journal and write down, in a step-by-step process, the events that drive them to do the things they do. It was good to see Willie again. He'd studied the bible with me some ten years earlier and was a good friend and mentor for spiritual matters. I'd never been able to write anything more than scribbling. I never could manage a clear thought on paper. But now I was motivated. I shut off the TV and sat down to go over my notes and to write down my thoughts about why I do what I do. My thoughts had always been so scattered, so many shadows of events.

Beatings and shouted curse words. Holidays ruined and violent family arguments and fist fights. Of being left with my father's friends, who raped me. Gang members, threats at gun point. I wrote until I lost all feeling in my hand, but I had written nothing about recent events.

My daughter came into the room and said, "Daddy, what is all of this?"

I looked up for the first time in hours at all the pages of legible writing. From midnight to eight in the morning, I had written page after page, the sheets of paper now spread all over the table and floor, some thirty-five pages.

What came first from my pen that night was the memory of my father's death and his funeral.

It was 1973 when my sister Linda burst through the double doors of my room, almost breaking the glass, franticly moaning and crying as though she were in pain. I sat up in bed as she flopped down beside me. Her hair in braids and wearing a flowered night shirt and a pair of denim shorts. I couldn't understand what she kept saying over and over. Then it became clear, "He's not coming back, he's not coming back."

"Sure he will," I said. "He always comes back, Tina (her nick name). He'll be back."

"No, he won't. Not this time. He's dead, he's dead. He won't be back."

This couldn't be true; it's some kind of sick joke. He could not have died. That just could not have happened.

I heard the family saying, "This was so sad, how he died, so sad." Others began to come in the room. "Well, Pete (my nickname). He's gone, what are we going to do?"

I thought, *what are we going to do? Celebrate! Are you crazy? Do you know what this means?* My mind was consumed. I was so happy! I don't know what they were all thinking; this wasn't a loss, not by a long shot. This man had done all kind of things to his wife and children. Had they forgotten all of this? They were crying and missing him as though he was a nice person or something. But he wasn't, he was evil.

I was fifteen, working in a production of the musical *Oliver* for a theatre group in Carson City. Rehearsals were long and hard, since there were so many small children in the production. They could only work for so many hours. The director split the rehearsals in two so half would rehearse the A.M. call and the other half would do the P.M. call. This meant the older cast members would run numbers with both groups. I played a character named Charlie; this character was in the London production, but not in the United States production. In addition to the part I played, my role basically consisted of keeping the younger kids motivated.

I was off for three days and returned home. Normally I didn't come home while in rehearsal, but this time for some reason I did. The days at home went by pretty quickly, and suddenly it was time for me to leave home to re-join the cast. My father was sitting on the sofa. He was listless and unusually quiet, even for him. His skin was an odd color, and his eyes were sunken in. He didn't look well, but he drank so much, he hadn't looked "well" in a very long time. We didn't speak to each other. That was the last time I would ever see him alive.

I was gone for another week, and when I returned home late one evening, the house was quiet. The boy's bedroom had changed a little. There was no longer a row of beds and a couple sets of twin beds. It was just Ed, my younger brother, and I in the room, and we slept in the twin beds. Our room was in the middle of the house. The previous owners had added on an additional room behind it, to create a family room. We had double glass doors on the room with a bamboo style curtain that kept the viewing blocked between the rooms. I came in and went to bed. A few hours later, I heard people talking and machines beeping and what sounded like crying. I guess I had just started to fall asleep when I saw two men pushing a bed past my bedroom door. My father was on the bed, and I heard one of the men say it was a heart attack. A heart attack was nothing new for him or us; he'd had three or four or five and would spend a week or so in the hospital and return home with the same negative, bad attitude as he had before. We always wished that he would not return; Mother would be better off without him. He was just a burden to her as he had gotten older.

I remember once when my mother was in the hospital for a month, she had prepared for us by stocking the refrigerator and the freezer with good food and meats. He made us eat black-eyed peas for a month while he fed his friends the stocked foods my mother had prepared. He would look at you with such distaste and disgust. To this day, I can't stand the smell or taste, let alone look at a black-eyed pea. I knew in my heart that if he died, she would be better off. That night as the bed rolled past my room, I knew he was not gone. He always came back after a heart attack. His attitude was sometimes worse, but never better. I lay back to close my eyes for what seemed like a few moments, but it was daylight when I awakened to the phone ringing, more people talking, and now crying and screaming.

Three days had gone by since his death, and I hadn't felt anything: no tears, no sorrow and no emotion. It was the day of the funeral, and the hearse and the limousines arrived to pick up the family. It was a warm, clear, quiet day; there hadn't been any days like this before he died. You could always look forward to rain or at least what seemed like a storm. But now it was quiet. The family entered the mortuary with tears. Except for knowing what the event of the day was to be, most of the family and friend's manner of dress looked as though they were going to church. The men wore black or dark colored suits and the women in black or dark colored dresses. The mortuary had the look of a small church, but the room looked like a scene from a Dracula movie. Heavy, dark red curtains draped the coffin from each side and candles flickered like lightning on the walls. I had a strange feeling that things would be different. The cock of the walk was gone.

There was the formality of passing by his body, person by person, to say our good-byes or, for me, to see if it was him in the coffin. He didn't look the same to me. The color of his skin was kind of a gray and pasty. He wore a dark suit and black tie, just as I had seen him wear to church and other funerals. His silver-gray hair was combed back as he had always worn it. The room was filled with sighs and tears and wailing. I saw my mother start to cry. I could only look at her, for I felt nothing. Dennis Lambert, a very tall six-foot-plus black man with black, short cropped hair and a big smile, was there for support. Dennis was always impeccably dressed and always chose his words correctly in his baritone New England manner of speech. He had been my junior high school music teacher. Now he was my friend and my personal manager. Mother had asked him to be a father to me. I sat next to him and across from the family who sat in the first three pews. He said it would be okay to cry for the loss. I had no loss, unlike my mother and the rest of them. Even if they didn't know it, they were better off. They were free.

At the burial site, my mother had bought a plot for two, one stacked on top of the other. The hole was very deep. After the service, everyone started to leave. I stayed to wait for the coffin to be lowered into the ground. I wanted to be sure. As they lowered the coffin, I thought I would only have to come here one more time when Mother died. But maybe we could persuade her not to be buried here. Then I would never return to these grounds. It was over. He and his friends were out of my life. He was gone, and they would have no reason to come to our home. My mother certainly did not drink or associate with them.

I remembered the first day he dropped me off at his friends' house. It was as though he gave me to them for their use. The fear I had and then the sickness, and then the pain as they took turns. There were always tears with no sound coming out of me. I could not let them know how much they were hurting me. The way my jaws hurt, and my throat was so sore. Then later in junior high school came the threats from that gang of boys and the man in the motel room, then the student from Washington High School. All that had happened to me. Did I ask for all of this? Was I just some punk, as he had called me, who deserved this?

The thought still brought about the smell and the feeling of sickness in my stomach. I could close my eyes and feel them on top of me, behind me, and inside me. They lowered the coffin into the ground and with it went any chance of my father ever saying he loved me. I still cry every time I see a loving scene in a film or on TV between a father and son. I guess I kept going back there with him because I hoped for a chance to be friends. I wanted him to love me like Mr. Feldman loved his sons, the way he held them and kissed them. Marty Feldman always wore suits and tie and a sweater. He was a man average in height with thick, black eyebrows and a full head of hair. He had such a calm voice that always made you feel welcome.

My father wore dark pants and a patterned short-sleeve shirt, roared and yelled, nothing calm about his voice. He would drop me at his friends at the curb, gesture for me to move away from the car. He'd blow his horn so they'd come out, take me to the front door, then he'd just drive away. By the time I walked up the stairs of that house and looked back, he was gone. The screen door would open and then the door to that room would close and lock. There would always be someone in that room waiting to molest, rape me, pants down, no clothes on. So many times, it had happened in that room with those men, his friends. His drunken friends. The match had been won years earlier when I refused to go back to that room. Now with his death, the game was over.

Chapter 2: Little Dancer

On September 1, 1957, Labor Day, I was born at the General Hospital just east of downtown Los Angeles, later re-named USC Medical Center. I was number ten of eleven children born to a laborer and a housekeeper. My father, in a previous marriage, had six children: Truman, Robert, Teta, Hayward, Georgia, and Lenabea. With my mother, there was Paul, August, Janice, Charles, Betty, Minnie, Anthony, Linda, Brenda, me, and Ed. My father's first marriage was to a Creole woman who was into magic and spells: voodoo. Rumor had it that if she handed you something, you could end up bewitched by one of her spells. My mother said on many occasions, "Make sure you never take anything from her, I don't trust her."

My father was a tall man, dark complexion with greyish eyes, about two hundred pounds and gray hair that he wore combed back. He smoked cigars, so his smell was a combination of soap and cigar smoke tossed in with a little gin or beer. It was said he was the cock of the walk, you know, a way with the ladies, at least by his friends. He was born in 1903 in Shreveport, Louisiana. He had completed only the third grade, but he could build and tear down any motor or engine. By the time I was born, he had an eye injury and was considered disabled. My mother was born in Beaumont, Texas in 1920. She was five-foot-ten, about one hundred and thirty pounds, red wavy hair with warm cinnamon-colored complexion as testimony to her Indian blood. Her scent was Channel Number Five. I'm sure one of the women she worked for gave her a sample of it, and that's all she wore from then on. She worked in wealthy homes as a housekeeper.

9

People always said, "You can eat off Maggie's floors." She was beautiful, quiet, and impeccable; a real lady.

My earliest memories of home, a large one story house with several bedrooms, each one with twin and bunk beds. The house sat on a large lot of land in the middle of the block. We had manicured front and back lawns with a few old trees that gave the house just enough shade in the summertime to keep it cool. My father was a stickler about the lawn; the grass was cut every two weeks, and every blade of grass had to be in place. The home furnishings were simple and clean, no clutter. The sofa and chairs were covered in plastic to protect them. The coffee and end tables were a dark wood, polished, no dust. We were not allowed to sit in the living room. You could pass through, but that's all, don't stop. The living room was for guests and the dining room was for dining. The den was a more comfortable room with its oversize furniture, and my father's favorite easy chair, a recliner with fabric on the arms, which we were not allowed to sit in. This was the family room. Not for flopping down, but sitting in. You could play a card game. The older kids could do their homework. Basically, for watching TV and a drink, water only, no juice or soda. If we wanted to be doing anything other than that, we'd be outside in the backyard. We weren't even allowed to be out in front of the house unless we were entertaining a guest. So, the sisters could entertain boyfriends if there wasn't too much noise.

We lived at 47th Street and Central Avenue. Just south of that area was a part of town where a good deal of black film stars and entertainers lived. The clubs they performed in and the theaters that showed the black films of the forties were there. Every so often someone would say, "That was So-and-So driving in that car. He used to be in that picture," or "She was a singer in her day." People still talked about the time they thought Sammy Davis Jr. was going to have a house in a nearby neighborhood.

It was a neighborhood of hard working people. Back then the men hung out at the barbershop telling fantastic stories of days gone by, usually hard to believe. Back then the women in the beauty parlor gossiped about who was doing it to whom and who was getting the two dollars. My mother would refer to them and say, "There used to be telegraph, then telephone, and then tell a woman." Moreover, of course, there was the corner drunk and the women who worked the corner.

People referred to us as "the little rascals" in the neighborhood. Not that we were mischievous, it was just that there were so many of us in the yard and on the porch. We were a tough-looking group, and the older boys were always into something, mostly fights. But I was a kid who always wore white or a light color. My mother had said, "White is like cleanliness, next to godliness," so I wore white. I did not like to be dirty.

My father one day, while changing the oil in his car, asked me to help. When the oil splashed on me, he yelled, "That's what men look like, we get dirty."

My father hated me. By the time I was four, I knew this. He often called me names: punk, fag. It was unusual for me to help him with anything because if I tried, he'd say, "Fag, you can't do nothing right." He took Ed with him everywhere, on trips or to the hardware store, gave him money to buy things; he'd show me when they returned.

Yet I was a punk, a fag. I didn't even know what that meant until a man who lived across the street came over and knocked on the door one evening. Chucky was a black man, very slim and dressed in flamboyant clothes and colors. He wore scarves that flowed in the wind behind him as he walked down the street, swaying from side to side. He had pierced ears with big hoop earrings dangling. He wore red lipstick and heavy eye make-up. In the evening, he dressed up as a woman. That was how he dressed when he worked. He looked like a girl, but he had muscles and better legs than most of the women who worked the corners.

I always thought he was funny. He had a great personality, and he was nice to the kids on the block, throwing back the ball when it went over his fence. Of course he threw like a girl, somewhat awkward. I always thought of him as just Chucky.

Chucky knocked on the door one night on his way out, and he was dressed as a woman. My father was sitting in the den watching TV, smoking a cigar, and drinking a beer. Ed and I were playing marbles on the floor. The second knock came a little harder. My father got up and looked out the window. The den was dark except for the light from the TV and the porch lights were off, so he couldn't see clearly. From the window, you could only see her shape and the hair. He said, "It's a woman, must be here for one of the girls." He was straightening himself up, tucking his shirt in with one hand while holding the beer can in the other.

As he opened the door, Ed and I went to the window. He turned on the light and saw that it was Chucky. "You. What you want?" Before Chucky could say a word, he slammed the door in his face and yelled, "Get away from my door, fag." He returned to the window. Peering through the blinds, he said, "Look how he walk. Look how he dressed; he a punk." Then he looked at me and said, "Just like you."

Chucky isn't like me. How can he see me in Chucky?

The rest of the night was devoted to how much he hated Chucky living in the neighborhood. How he was an eye sore to real men and punk this and sissy that, and all this was directed at me.

Holidays, weekends, and birthdays were the worst of all. My father was not sentimental. On our birthday, he'd give us special attention, but not a good kind. He'd say, "Your birthday, huh? The day you were born, I got another mouth to feed. Just because it's your birthday, you still nothing and gonna be nothing."

My mother made us a cake and told us we were special. We were special to her from the time she went to the hospital to deliver. She did her hair and make up so that when we arrived, she would be beautiful. The staff at the hospital always thought she was there for some other reason. They said, "Are you here to deliver or what?" She did her best to create a special memory for every holiday and birthday, not an easy task with eleven children.

My father always ruined those special occasions by saying, "You'll never be nothing." I don't know how many times I heard him say that to all of us, except for Ed, his youngest son. Somehow Ed was to be something. He was dad's favorite and spoiled. One word of disapproval or not getting his way, he would tell his dad, and that would result in a whipping or at least a backhand slap across the room. Mr. Ed would whine if no attention was being paid to him or if his dad had promised him money and had not given it to him. Once he promised him a quarter, and Ed kept asking for it. Dad was with his friends and told him to wait, but Ed continued to ask for it. Ed grabbed for his pocket, and Dad backhanded him across the room and yelled, "I told you to wait." That was the only time I ever saw Ed get hit. Usually Tony or I got that reaction.

Dad's favorite TV show was pro wrestling. He would take us out back to the yard and pit us against each other to see which one would come out on top. This was not for play, this fight was real. For the most part, I wouldn't fight Ed, or at least I tried not to hurt him because hurting him could get me hurt.

My mother called me into her bedroom. She said, "I hate to say this to you, but if you fight or don't fight you are still going to get a whipping. You may as well fight and kick his butt because that's the only whipping he's going to get."

She was right. I always got a whipping afterwards, so I fought; I bloodied his nose. I got beat with the electrical cord, the "Sting A Ree," as it was called, for giving Ed a bloody nose.

To this day, Ed and I don't have a relationship. We aren't friends, we don't associate with each other, and we have never even been to each other's homes. He called me once. I didn't even recognize his voice. We rarely see each other at Mom's house on holidays. I don't hold it against him; it was his father who did this, but things have never changed.

That was how the family functioned. We loved each other, but sometimes it seemed like from a distance. When we're together now, we laugh and seemingly have a good time, but everyone is protected in his or her own space.

My mother worked in Beverly Hills and Hollywood for actors and studio types. She maintained the housekeeping and cooking staff at their parties: Jack Warner, Dan Daily, the Andersen's, the Ore's, and others. She didn't drive, so she had a bus trip from Forty-seventh and Central in Los Angeles, where we lived, hours and three or four bus transfers to where she worked.

My father hardly ever drove her or picked her up from work. He stayed busy sitting in his chair watching TV Westerns and occasionally, sending someone to get him some water. We'd run up the block to meet her at the bus stop to help her with the six or seven bags of groceries, like a pack horse she'd be carrying.

There was one occasion when Dad, Ed, and I drove to Hollywood to pick her up from work. That was rare because he never let me go anywhere with them. We arrived early, which was his custom, but he was an hour earlier than he needed to be, so he waited impatiently, as was also his custom. He began to get upset and started to curse and slam his hands on the steering wheel. He sent me after her, "Go get your mother. She's in there working for these white folks now, and I gotta sit here and wait for her." He didn't work and most of the time didn't speak to anyone. Monday through Thursday mornings, he barely said ten words. By Thursday evening, he was drunk and then talked through Saturday night, cursing and telling us that we would 'never be nothing.' Sunday, he was off to the Catholic Church for confession.

The Dailey house was huge, with a circular driveway, a lawn that went on forever, and trees and beautiful wood doors with beveled glass. As I came to the door, a man stepped outside, "Are you here for Maggie?"

"Yes, I am."

He smiled and put his hands on my shoulders. He looked me in the eye and said, "You're pretty sharp. She's out back; go around this way."

I walked down the side of the house in awe the whole time at the size of it. It seemed endless. When I got around back, it was more beautiful than a movie: the pool, the grounds, and the tennis court. I thought, *Wow, what a house*, as I stood there with my mouth open. *Beverly Hills, this is how all the movie stars live.* Big houses and grounds that looked like a brand-new park, only better.

My sisters used to always tell a story of our lives, that we were rich. They never said how we became so rich. We just kind of woke up and were rich. The house they described looked like the Dailey house. The only difference was we lived there. Their make-believe world was always referred to as "The Story." We'd all gather around when my father was out and listen to the story.

Another man sat at a table in the back. He got up and came over to me. He was tall and slim with dark blonde hair and dressed in a suit, no tie, but an ascot around his neck. He said, "You like this place?"

I said, "It's beautiful."

He said, "Step up here so you can get a better look. You're here for Maggie?"

"Yes, I am."

"Come on in, I'll let her know you're here." As he stepped away, he started to dance. He looked over his shoulder. "What do you think of that step?" I copied his steps. He said, "Well, what do you know. Do this." He moved from side to side, did some footwork. "Now you do it." He watched me. "Where did you pick this up?"

I told him I watched a lot of TV, a lot of dancers like Fred Astaire, Gene Kelly and the ladies, Ann Miller, Judy Garland. I said, "And that Dan Dailey, he's great with Betty Grable. He doesn't look like a dancer, but he's great."

"He doesn't, huh, but you really like him?"

"Yes, I do."

He chuckled and left me to get my mother. When they returned, he said, "Watch this, Maggie. Do this." A time step. I did it. "Maggie, what do you know, he's a dancer."

"Yes, he is," my mother said. "Come on, little dancer, we have to go."

"By the way, what's your name, little dancer?"

"Donn," I said.

"I'm Dan."

I held out my hand, "Nice to meet you, Dan."

He laughed, "Nice to meet you, Donn."

"Come on, you," my mother said. "Bye, Mr. D."

"Bye, Maggie."

"We don't want to keep your father waiting any longer. You know how he is, and don't tell him you were dancing with Mr. D. That'll make him mad."

"Okay, Mom."

As we got to the car she said, "I think Dan Dailey likes the way you copied his steps."

"Dan who?" I said.

"Dailey," she said, "the actor."

My mouth froze open.

My father yelled, "Get in the car, fool."

Chapter 3: "Punk, Fag": A Father's Words

At age five, I went to school, Ascot Elementary. It was great to get out of the house. I sat directly behind my father as he drove me to school in his late-fifties gun-grey Buick. The seats were kind of striped light and dark blue. "I'm going to take you the first day, but after this, you on your own; you'll have to walk." We left early, as usual, and arrived to watch the other cars pull up, parents getting out, holding their kids' hands, walking them to the gate of the school. There were mostly black kids and a few whites and Latinos and even a couple of Asians. I had not seen that before in our neighborhood. He looked at me and said, "Get out the car, and I don't want to get no bad reports on you, and I don't want to get no calls from your teacher about you."

The street was slightly tilted where we parked. I tried to push open the car door, but it was so heavy, it slammed closed. By the third time, he jumped out of the car and opened it. "Now get out." I crossed the street thinking he was behind me. As I got close to the other curb, I heard the car door slam. I walked to the gate and turned to look back. He was gone. The teachers stood at the gate greeting the parents. One turned to me and asked, "Where are your parents?" I said nothing. She took my hand and walked me and the other kids into the classroom.

I had heard my brothers and sisters talk about school. The guys hated it, and the girls liked it, for the most part. They liked the teachers and hated the homework. The teacher let me help her with everything: passing out papers, paint, and our paint shirts so we wouldn't spill paint on our clothes. It was so

17

much better than being at home with nothing to do. At home I was alone, but at school we were all having fun.

By the second week, I'd become the teacher's helper. I would arrive early each day to help set up the day's activities. I stood at the gate with her to greet the parents, passing out the information sheets about what was needed or expected.

About the fourth week of school, a new student arrived, Angela. Standing at the end of the line with a tall, thin man dressed in a dark business suit and hat was a beautiful girl with a great big smile. She wore a yellow dress with a white collar and a white belt. Her yellow socks with white lace trim were perfectly folded at the ankle to complement her white, shiny shoes. She wore her blonde hair parted down the middle and braided. Her bangs were cut just above her green eyes.

All the other girls in the class were just ordinary, but Angela was something special. She arrived by car with her father each day. He would get out of the car, then walk around and open her door for her, take her by the hand as she exited the car, and then he would close her door, kiss her, and hug her goodbye. He'd say, "I'll be here to pick you up."

Every day all the students arrived with their parents, and at the end of the parade were Angela and her father. I always said good morning to him, and he would say, "And a good morning to you." One morning he added, "Would you take care of my little girl?" Sure, I will…

From then on, we played together every day. We were paint partners and did all our little projects together. I was happy at school with Angela and the teacher and with all the kids. After watching Angela's father, the teacher said it would be a good idea if we all learned to open doors for ladies, well girls, and hold their chairs while they sat down. Of course, there were more girls than boys, so some guys had to do it for more than one girl. I told the teacher what Angela's father had asked of me, to take care of his little girl, so I always held Angela's chair. After a few weeks, I told my mother about her. She said, "Don't let your father know about her; you know how he feels about white people." I thought he would be happy she was a girl. "Yeah, but she a white girl," my mother would say. "Let's just keep this between you and me." But I had already told Ed, and he would tell his dad.

It was the spring semester, and in class we began to draw pictures of hearts and flowers. We were going to make Valentine's Day cards for our parents.

The teacher said we were going to draw names, and we could buy or make a special card for our favorite classmate. Some girls had to do two. I did not draw Angela's name nor she mine, but we had made a deal that we'd do something special for each other. I asked my mother to buy me a special card to give to Angela. It had been a few days, and she was home early from work, still wearing her maid's uniform from a garden party. She brought out a box of cards and handed them to me. She said I should give them to all the kids, not just one. I told her, okay, but I needed something a little special for Angela. She went to her room and came out with a brown paper bag and handed it to me. "Will this work?"

I opened the bag and pulled out a beautiful white card with a red fabric heart that folded out and said, "You're Special." It was perfect. I hugged her and told her Angela would love it.

My mother stood over me as I sat at the table in the dining room and wrote out all the kids' names on each card. I wanted to write something in private on Angela's card, so I left the other cards on the table and went to my room. After gathering my thoughts, I finished the card, placed it in the envelope, and put it back in the bag. Then I put it under my pillow.

I returned to the table to get the other cards, but Ed had them in his hands, and my father was standing at the table. He took the cards from Eddie.

"What are these?"

I said, "Valentine's Day cards. I'm going to give them to the girls in my class."

"You don't like girls, you a punk fag." He took the cards and tore them up. And he threw them on the floor. Ed smirked and said, "He likes girls, Dad. He got a girlfriend. She got green eyes and she white too."

My father slammed his hand down on the table and grabbed me by the arm. "No, he don't," he declared. "You a punk. Get out of my face." I got a whipping and sent to my room.

After the spanking, I was told to clean up the mess. I went to my bedroom which was shared with two other brothers. The room was a pretty nice size; it had two twin beds and a set of bunk beds up against the wall and three four-drawer dressers. Each of my brothers had a drawer, and Ed and I shared two drawers each. I was sitting on the bed, and I had the top bunk. My mother came in. "I wish you hadn't left those on the table," she said.

"Yeah, Mom. Me, too."

"You know how he is."

"I know, Mom."

She hugged me and as she was leaving the room she said, "What about the special one?"

I smiled. "I have it. It was under my pillow."

She smiled and winked. "Good."

On Thursday the fourteenth, I arrived early and told the teacher what had happened. She went to her desk and pulled out a box of cards. "You have time to write the names on them," she said.

All the kids arrived and we began passing out cards to each other, but Angela had not yet arrived. Ten minutes, fifteen minutes had passed; they were always the last to arrive, but never this late. I went back outside the gate to see if I saw their car. I waited five minutes, and then the car pulled up. Angela did not wait for her father to open the door. She just jumped out and ran over to me. Her father came running over too. "We're late today." He kissed her and turned to leave. "Oh, thanks for taking care of my little girl. She has a little something special for you."

Angela and I turned to go into the gate and looked at each other and laughed because we had planned a special something for each other, our personal cards. It was a great day.

Kindergarten was over so fast. It was June, and school was ending for the summer break. We had a party, and I found out that Angela would not be back in September. Her family was moving. We all said our goodbyes, and I watched as Angela got into her father's car and drove away for the last time.

School became my refuge, a place where I was safe with teachers who liked me and kids I could have fun with. In first grade, I had a new teacher, Miss Jenkins. She was young and beautiful, with dimples, jet-black hair, and a talent for singing and music. Not only was she the first-grade teacher, but also the piano instructor, and she was in charge of the chorus. I would often stay after school, and she would talk to me about acting and singing. We would read and act out the different parts in the plays. While the other kids were on the playground after school, I spent all my time in her classroom. She'd say, "You should become an actor. You can do it; you really can do it."

On weekends she would take me to a theater company she was working with. They were auditioning for different parts in the plays for their summer season. She said, "See how it's done, it's not that hard. Just read your part. Don't worry about the lines, just react to what's being said."

One afternoon I was sitting in the den watching TV when the news said President John F. Kennedy had been killed. My father stood up and said, "One less white man." He scowled at all the people on the news, the sadness on their faces, the crying. He didn't even like the President. He started talking about how Kennedy didn't care for the colored people, just for the rich. It was another one of his drinking weekends, and the entire weekend was devoted to how much he thought Kennedy was nothing but just another one of those white folks who had everything.

I'm sure he must have experienced prejudice, being born at the top of the century. It was the sixties now, and prejudice was still strong, but not for me. My teachers were mostly white, and the white people I met were nice to me. The people my mother worked for were nice. She never said anything bad about the way they treated her. But he hated them, all of them. To him, no white person was good.

One morning when I arrived at school, a lot of strange people were buzzing around. One of the teachers told me they were interviewing students about family and friends and asking them to tell little stories. They wanted to see who was friendly and outgoing. They had chosen quite a few of the children to come to the multipurpose room. It was a palpable feeling of excitement going around; these people were from television and they wanted children for some TV show. They just asked a few questions, and that was it. They wanted to see if we had a personality. They wanted children with great personalities.

At the end of the day, I was called to the office. They said they needed to get permission from my parents and that I had been chosen to go on the show. They would call my home within the next hour or so. I couldn't believe they had chosen me. The women in the office were saying, "You got it!"

I was excited at first, then I thought, "Oh no, they're going to call home. I've got to get there before they call, before the phone rings, or I'm going to be in trouble." I ran from the school building and all the way home. Just as I got there, the phone rang and rang, but no one picked up. My mother was in the bathroom, and the phone stopped ringing. He was there, but didn't pick up.

I came through the door, and he yelled, "Why are you running in this house?"
I was out of breath. I said, "I was just in a hurry to get in. Where's Mom?"
He looked up. "She's in the bathroom."
The phone rang and he grabbed it. "Hello!"
It was the school calling. He never answered the phone. By the end of the first grade, the school had been calling home about me. All good reports, but my mother always answered it. This time they were calling to say I had been chosen to go on the "Art Linkletter Show," and he had to answer the phone.

When the caller mentioned my name, he hung up, slamming the phone down. He turned to me, "I told you I did not want to get no calls about you!"

He grabbed me, crushing my shoulder, and began to threaten me with a beating. The phone rang again, and this time my mother picked it up in her room. He had just begun hitting me when she ran into the room.

"The school is calling! They say he's a good student and he's been chosen to go on TV. The Art Linkletter Show."

He let go of me and walked away, mumbling.

The next day everyone was talking about it. All the neighbors were congratulating him. That made him happy. He was the talk of the block. His friends were calling, and he was answering the phone, tickled that his son was going to be on TV. I thought, maybe it's been me all this time. Maybe I hadn't given him a chance to like me.

I had never gone with him to his friends' homes, and now he was asking me to come along. It was finally happy around the house. He was joking. People made jokes about him not talking all week except for the weekends, and he laughed. It was unbelievable how everything had changed.

It was the day of the event. He had stopped driving me to school since the first day nearly two years ago. On this day, he drove me to school early. A limousine was parked in front of the school with a large man waiting outside of the car, kind of pacing back and forth. Dad said, "He must be your driver." Like having a driver meet me at school with a limo was a common occurrence. He got out of the car and walked me to the gate of the school.

By then the other kids started coming out, checking out the car. I was happy to have him walk me to the car. The other parents were there with their kids. The driver opened the door, and the other kids started to get into the car. I looked back to see him as he drove away. I got in, and the driver closed the door.

Hollywood was supposed to be a place where dreams come true. I was finally in the place where Fred Astaire, Judy Garland, and Dan Dailey were. A magical place where I could forget about all the things that was so bad at home. I was going to be on television and have a shot. As my teacher always said, "If you get your shot, you have a chance."

Seeing such a place in those days was something else. They didn't show a lot of "behind the scenes" as they do now, so what we saw that day was new and amazing. The driver got to the gate of the studio, and the guard waved him in. We were escorted to a place they called the green room, where we would wait for a person to talk to us about what we were going to do. The room was not quite green, so we were all a little confused and laughed at the lady who said it was green. Everyone we met was so nice. They set up games for us to play. They walked us around, showing the different rooms where things took place.

I was looking for Fred and Judy and Dan and the others I had seen on TV. It seemed so strange. I thought about the people at the studio. All these people were white and nice, not at all like my father said they would be. No one was pushing us around and calling us names. They treated us great. They took us to meet Art Linkletter, the man himself, and he was a gentleman. Mr. Linkletter was a large man with dark hair combed back from his nice face. He was your typical grandfather-like character. He had been in television for a long time. He joked with us and asked if we had other names that family members used that we would prefer to be called.

We were escorted to some chairs and a large room. They had people fussing over us in the chairs. We were on the set. "Make sure he's in the light," a voice said. I could hear voices but couldn't see anyone because the lights were blinding. I could feel people moving around back and forth. Mr. Linkletter went down the line shaking hands with everyone, preparing us for the show, letting us know that it was about to start, and that we were going to have some fun. In the green room, the kids were talking and having fun, but when we sat in those chairs on set, everyone got quiet and stiff in a way. This was it. We were on.

Mr. Linkletter went down the line of chairs talking to each of the kids, asking question about family and friends, and what things we liked to do. I began to think, my mind raced. I hoped he wouldn't ask me about my family. What could I say? I couldn't speak of the drunken violence. He was coming to me. He stepped in front of me. This was my shot, this was my shot, this was my shot. I kept hearing this in my head over and over. What could I say? Then it hit me.

Talk about my sister Betty and the boys she dated. She and her girlfriends always got a big laugh when they created stories about not being available when one guy called because she was already out with another. So, that's what I talked about. I didn't know she was lying to them and that this was a secret between her and her girlfriends. The audience roared with laughter, and Mr. Linkletter laughed and slapped his leg. It was great, I was funny, what I had said was funny. Something about being in front of that audience was electrical. It gave me a feeling unlike anything I had felt before.

As he went past me to the next kid, I could now see the audience. They were all white and laughing, having fun with these kids. I knew then my father was wrong. It was he, not the rest of the world, who had a problem. I had found people who were fun, who enjoyed humor, and something came over me that was warm and comforting, a feeling of safety, a feeling that it was going to be all right, that nothing could hurt me anymore. The audience gave me a sense of belonging somewhere. It's like the world opened and said "You're okay." I was not a punk or a fag, just one of the other kids. I don't know what the other kids felt, but on that stage, I was home.

The show was over, and we were told that we were going to be taken to lunch at a big, fancy restaurant. The limousine arrived, we got in and off to the restaurant we went. The day was so perfect that I would not forget this day for as long as I lived. Television, Art Linkletter, and an audience my body would ache for, and my soul would long for all the days of my life.

The return to school was wild. The teachers and the students cheered as they gathered around. "How was it? How was the studio? How is Art Linkletter? Did you see all the stars in the movies?" It was crazy, frantic, and silly in a fun, fantastic way. All these people wanting my attention. Wanting to know what I knew. When I got to my classroom, Miss Jenkins just stood there and smiled. She took me by the hand and walked me to her desk. "Well, this is what you have to look forward to. People will want to know how it is and how it was, and what do you think about things."

There were students looking through the window of the classroom. What were they looking at, it was just me. It was great. They wanted to know, and I wanted to tell them. We laughed and talked about the experience and what it had meant to me.

They'd said they would notify us as to when it would air. Things at home had improved with the news of the show, and my father was still the talk of the neighborhood. He drank, but it was a celebration more than the normal violent, soggy drama that usually took place. When we got a call that the show was coming on, everyone was notified, our neighbors and friends and his friends.

They'd been asking me what I had said on the show, but I would never say, and my mother would say, "Wait until the show, then we can all hear together."

Now the show was on, and everyone was in the living room talking and watching. And there I was. Art Linkletter in front of me, and I started talking. The audience was in laughter, the house was in laughter, the neighbors were laughing through the windows in their homes. Betty, my sister, was not laughing. Her boyfriend was not laughing, and my father was not laughing at all.

He looked at me, got up and walked away from the TV. Then the rest of the family was caught up in laughter and soon my sister's boyfriend was laughing, too. She said to me, "Next time, pick on someone else, okay?" The neighbors congratulated my father; he was still the big man in the neighborhood.

It was good while it lasted.

Chapter 4: Shave and a Haircut, Two Bits

The atmosphere in the house soon returned to being a nightmare as he became a drunken terror. Our fear made us hate him, his friends, his ranting. and ravings. It was constant.

One Thanksgiving, Mother spent several days preparing for the holiday. She made six pies and seven cakes. The food she prepared, these desserts, she made from scratch, no box pre-made. She laid it out on the table. Well, not quite a table; there were so many of us, we had sort of a park-bench table. She was ready to serve and called him to the table. It was now the third or forth time she had called. He came to the table, cursed everyone out, and said that we did not deserve what she had made. He said to her, "I told you to wait." He lifted the table and turned everything onto the floor and into our laps.

We all saw the look on her face, the tears. She was so hurt. He swaggered off to rejoin his friends who told him that he shouldn't have done that, but he told them to shut up and they did. They were afraid of him and backed down quickly. Later that night, it would turn out to be the best Thanksgiving ever. He and his friends laughed as they talked about the look on her face and the food all over the floor. One of them said, "You're still the strongest man around, no one could take you on."

Well, Mom had heard enough. Normally when he went on these tantrums, she would clean every pot, pan, wall, floor, counter-top, and appliance in the house. That's how she got the reputation for having floors you could eat off. This time she started throwing the pots and pans at him and his friends. She was wild. The kids all starting cheering. Well, he was not going to be embarrassed in front of his friends, so he went for her, but her brother Chester stepped in to keep him from her.

Chester had been in the Navy since he was 17. Mother was older and had signed him into the Navy. She'd always taken care of him. Chester was tall and skinny, about one-hundred-thirty pounds, and kept his military look about himself. Haircut and just the way he carried himself, very Navy. He was also no match for the cock of the walk, who knocked him down and wrestled him to the floor. His friends cheered even more as he punched Chester again and again. Then in a rage, he went for her again. Us kids were now crying and screaming. The house was in turmoil; the neighbors were now all standing out in front of the house. I remember the look on her face as she turned to look at her children. She was terrified. She looked like she'd been wrapped and smothered in fear.

He went for her; she turned towards him, and from somewhere in her, she swung her fist from the floor up and landed a punch that knocked him off his feet, through the door, and onto the porch. He was dazed, on his back, and bleeding. His friends started to pick him up. She yelled at them. I had never heard her raise her voice.

"Pick him up," she shouted, "and get out of my house!" She started throwing his clothes out the door. We were cheering, now the neighbors were cheering, and it was something else. How did she do this to the cock of the walk? He was on his ass, and she was standing over him. He would never attack her again. Everything else he did would now be in secret.

By now most of the older brothers and sisters were gone from the house. Tony was tall and skinny and would always stay out past the dinner hour. He was told if he missed the dinner call, he wouldn't eat. One night he came in late for dinner and didn't realize it was a Thursday and that he was going to meet the wrath of Dad's drinking. He got nothing to eat and was knocked across the room, then was talked to for hours into the early morning. Then Dad gave him a dollar and a dime.

"Take this dollar and go downtown to Fifth Street with the rest of them bums, and when you had enough, take that dime, buy yourself a rope and hang yourself because you will never be nothing." Tony curled his lip in a smirk and ran out of the house. He soon joined a gang. He would travel with the wrong crowd for the rest of his life, in and out of jail until the time of his death. In the early nineties, he was released from prison. He had met a lady who studied the bible with him, and they were to be married. On their way to Mom's house from Lancaster to Los Angeles for an introduction of his fiancée, their car went off a cliff. It dropped over a hundred feet, and they were both killed. In life, Tony would experience failure and tragedy because of a father who did not love him and a mother who loved, but was powerless against her husband. In death, Tony would have the last laugh when he was buried in a plot purchased for two, one on top of the other. Tony would end up on top of the father who hated him.

The girls in the family did not escape tragedy. His damage to them would cause most of them to turn to alcohol, drugs, hating, and distrusting of men. This abuse went on until his death. It would be years before the girls could speak to Mother about what was going on. She cried and said to them, "I was afraid. What was I to do?" I realize now that I was fortunate. Through whatever gifts God gave me, I was able to overcome the trauma and find my way.

It had been almost a year since the TV show. I was eight years old. My father said that on the weekend he would be going to his friends' house and that he wanted me to go. He usually only took Ed with him, and now I was invited. Maybe the show had made a difference.

Well, Thursday began the drinking through Friday, and by Saturday he was still drinking. It was 11:00 in the morning, and he said it was time to go meet up with his friends. This was scary. He was and was not his usual self; it was hard to tell. He was not cursing at or about something. Ed and I got in the back seat, he backed out of the driveway, and off we went. Although there was a radio in the car, a Philco my father never played music or ever turned it on. On the way there, he was quiet. Except for some talking under his breath which we didn't understand, not words just grunting and shaking his head from side to side. Ed and I played and joked, but he didn't say much. It was about a thirty-minute drive, and Ed asked if we could roll down the windows because it was such hot day. We arrived at the house, and he sounded the horn in his usual manner (shave and a haircut, two bits). He got out of the car as the men started coming out of the house and off the porch. The men who emerged from the house were tall and fat, and some were short and just ugly. They all seemed drunk. He told Ed to get out and come on over to the guys. Ed knew these guys; he'd been with him quite a few times before.

He looked at me and said, "You sit there, we'll be back." I sat in the car for a half hour, sweating in my white pull over shirt and cream colored shorts while they were all inside. I thought, is this it? Is this what it's like to go with them to be around his friends?

Then my father, with all of them, came out of the house and over to the car. They were talking in that drunk slurring of words and pointing at me and laughing. (He's on TV, punk, sissy, let me see him) Something had changed. I rolled up the window. "Get out of the car, punk." He opened the door and pulled me out by the arm. "This is my son, the sissy, the punk, and he thinks because he's been on TV, he's something. Well, you're not, you still a punk."

He pulled me up the stairs to the house and pushed me toward the door. I tripped and fell into one of the guys and then to the floor just inside the door. They laughed. I looked up to see inside the house. The place was so filthy, and the smell was unbelievable. Like the smell of cigar, cigarettes, booze, and a gas station restroom, all rolled into one. The roaches—big ones, little ones, all over the place. Dirty clothes, dishes with old food on them on the floor. It was terrible. The furniture was ripped open, the cotton hanging out onto the floor. The fabric on the arms of the sofa was open to expose the wood. And the pillows looked as though someone had attempted to fix them, but didn't know what they were doing. The stitches were too wide and revealed the cotton inside. The carpet had large holes in it, as though something had eaten through it to the wood floors. The chairs and coffee table had broken legs and were held up with wood blocks. There were torn bed sheets on the windows for curtains. The screens were pulled away and the glass broken out of some of the window. This was where he and Ed went on weekends?

One of the guys picked me up and held me to him. I thought I was going to be sick. My father said, "Put him down someplace out of my face."

A big fat man said, "Put him in that room, there's a TV in there, and you can lock the door."

Lock the door, I thought, what for? My father said, "Get in there and sit down or something; just get out of my face. I don't want to see you or hear

30

you." I started to cry. He slapped the back of my head. "No crying." The door closed, and then it locked. I could hear them cursing and yelling. This went on for about an hour.

The room was dimly lit with light from the bathroom. There was a bedspread for curtains hung on the windows. The TV was sitting on a milk crate in the corner of the room. It was on, but the tube was going out, and it was almost black. I leaned on a sofa bed that was half open, the pillows thrown across the floor. I did not want to sit on anything in that room. It was as dirty as the living room, with clothes and things thrown everywhere and the smell of old food. The bathroom had no door on it. I looked in, and it was just like the gas stations, but it had a bathtub that was dirt black with roaches crawling all around.

Why did he bring me here to leave me in this room? I could not understand this. I kept hearing the front screen door slamming. It had been about an hour or so, and the sounds in the other room had gotten quieter. Soon there were no sounds out there at all. Just as I moved toward the bedroom door to listen for voices, it was unlocked and shoved open, and the fat man who picked me up at the top of the steps stood in the doorway. I jumped back from the door. He looked to me about seven feet tall, with a bald head and yellow skin. He wore no shirt, and his chest was hairy, with marks all over him. And the smell. He smelled like dirty feet and sour milk.

He closed the door and yelled, "Everyone went to the liquor store. It's just you and me." He tripped over the sofa, and then staggered into the bathroom. He turned and stared at me while he unzipped his pants. He stood there for a while holding himself, and then he turned to the toilet. While he urinated, he said, "I'm a friend of your dad's. Your dad says you're a punk, a sissy." He turned from the toilet and began rubbing and pulling on himself. "There is something you sissies like to do for us men. I want you to do it. I'm going to give you something."

He came toward me, still holding himself. "Are you a punk, boy?" He came closer; the smell was getting worse. He stood in front of me, right at my face just inches away. "You'd like this, boy, wouldn't you? Come on, boy, come on." He moved closer and put it to my lips. I moved back. "Come on, boy, no one's here. Just you and me." He put his hand on the back of my neck and pulled my head to it. The taste and the smell were so bad. It was warm, a cream-like, that filled my mouth. "You come here. You should be able to do this for us guys when you come here. Nobody's gonna hurt you if you open your mouth and do what we just did." He pulled my shirt over my head and wiped himself. He handed me the shirt. Then he pushed me backwards onto the sofa. He left the room and closed the door and locked it. My neck and my jaws were sore. I sat back up on the arm of the sofa.

It had been quiet in the outer room for a while, then I heard a voice say, "You're right, Bee, [my fathers name] he a punk. He don't like to do what men like." My father said nothing.

I tried to turn the doorknob, but it was locked. I looked at the stain and the dark marks on my shirt. I began to cry. How was I going to change my clothes? I thought maybe I could wash it off. I hated being dirty. Why would he bring me to this dirty place? I walked over to look into the bathroom. I couldn't go in there, it made me sick. The only place in the room with water was that bathroom, and I was not going in there. Everyone would see the stains on my shirt, on my clothes.

An hour later, the door was unlocked. I was told to come out and go to the car. My father stopped me as I came out of that room. "See, you ain't no big shot. You a punk. Nobody here think you something because you been on TV. You don't fit in with us men. Now you won't ask to come back here if you have to sit in that room and do nothing all day. Nobody here gonna spend time with you. Ed's a man like us, you ain't."

I walked outside the front door. I could see the stains more clearly now. I hated to be dirty. We drove home, and I thought he might say something about the day to me, but all he continued to do was curse and say I was a punk and a fag.

That evening he took out a dollar and gave it to Ed. He turned to me and said, "Get out of my face." He and Ed walked to the front door. I went around to the back of the house and sat on the porch. I pulled the shirt off. I would rather wear nothing than to wear that dirty shirt. I still had that taste in my mouth and that smell in my nose. I went into the bathroom and put soap in my mouth, and then I took a bath. The next morning, I took another bath. I couldn't get the taste and smell off me.

Chapter 5: Washing, Ironing, and Auditioning

We moved to another part of the city, and I changed schools. I would miss Miss Jenkins—the way she made me feel, her smile, her warmth. Would there be another teacher like her at the new school? When I returned to school after being at that house, she was so nice. She said she had watched me all through class and something had changed. She said she knew I couldn't tell her, but if I wanted to it would be okay. She just held me after class one day and told me I would be safe. It's as though she knew, but how could she?

Our new house was too far away for me to walk and meet her at her theater class, so I wouldn't be able to spend weekends with her anymore either. I had just turned eight and was attending Raymond Avenue Elementary School. I was in the third grade; Mrs. Miller was my new teacher. It was so strange walking into her classroom. When she turned around from the board, she looked just like Miss Jenkins. Same color hair and same smile. She asked me to come in and take a seat. She told the students that I was new and from another school and that I had been on TV. And she told them I had been studying acting at a theater in Los Angeles and that I had a great singing voice, and then she introduced me to everyone. How did she know all of this? She sat me next to a beautiful girl with long, brown braids in her hair.

"Her name is Eyvonne, she's going to show you around. By the way, your teacher Miss Jenkins is a friend of mine."

33

Eyvonne was nice. She took me to the break area and introduced me to all the other kids. Everyone asked me about TV; even though it had been a year or so, the fascination was still there. When school was over for the day, I asked Eyvonne if I could walk her home. As we walked, I noticed we were going in the same direction as my house. She lived at 77th and Vermont, and I lived at 78th, just around the corner. The back fences to our yards were joined. We walked to and from school every day.

It had been almost three months; I had not mentioned her to anyone at home. I hadn't forgotten what happened when my father found out about Ingrid. When the school year was over for summer break, I would go down the block and around the corner, never through the fence, to Eyvonne's house. I didn't want anyone to know where I was going, especially Ed. Eyvonne was kind of a girlfriend, and I wanted to protect her and me from the remarks that my father might make.

My birthday came, and school was about to start. One Friday evening, as usual, my father was at his worst. The sun was going down. At my house, that meant you were supposed to be inside the house. I was still out back and wanted to see Eyvonne before the day was over. There was no time to make the trip around the corner, so I decided to go through the fence. My father came out the back door just in time to see me disappear through the fence and followed me. He saw me talking to Eyvonne at her garage, and we were holding hands.

He called out to me, "Hey, boy!"

I told her I better go; I'd see her on the way to school. When I got to the fence and stepped through, he was standing there. "So that where you been going, with some little girl? You musta forgot you don't like girls."

I said, "I like her, she's nice."

He slapped my face. "You're a fag."

One of my best friends in school was David Black. We were at his house playing one afternoon, and I asked him if he had started to do it yet, but he didn't know what I was talking about. Maybe I wasn't explaining it right. I thought, maybe he hasn't started yet. I talked about the smell of it, I tried to tell him how much his jaws would hurt. He just laughed and said he was strong and would be able to take it. I wasn't sure we were talking about the same thing. Whenever I went to the boys' restroom, I tried to make sure I was the only one there. The sounds of other boys using the bathroom made me sick. The man in the room had said I was the right age to this for them. I wondered if anyone else had yet. We were all about the same age.

My father came in the house one Saturday. He was drunk and said he was going for the day and that I was going with him and Mr. Ed. I told him that he didn't have to take me if he didn't want to, I would stay home. He yelled, "Shut up, you're going! It's just us men and you."

I was put into that dirty room. The smells were the same that I remembered. I heard my father and another man talking. "I was gonna leave him at home, but if you want him here with us men while we're drinking… When us guys go out to the liquor store, he's just gonna sit in that room by himself. I don't wanna have to look at him, but it's your house."

The man said, "Well, I gotta leave somebody here to watch the house, he'll be okay; we'll lock the door. You guys go and pick up the drinks."

My father was saying, "Just leave him here, you don't have to stay. I can sit here while he's in there. You're no fag babysitter." They went back and forth for a while. I could hear the beer cans being opened and more voices and the front screen door being opened and slammed shut.

It had been about an hour or so when I heard someone say, "Bee, we ain't gonna all fit in the car, so while Mr. Ed and the other kids are next door playing, you guys go and I'll stay, finish this bottle, and keep an eye on Hat." Hat was one of the old drunks, passed out on the sofa. The other voices agreed, "Let's go, Bee."

I heard the house emptying out. The screen door kept slamming. It was quiet again in the outer room.

The door opened; the yellow skinned man came in the room and old Hat with him. He yelled, "Well, you got a little bigger than you was last time you was here. That's even better; you can take it better now." He began to open his pants. He said to the other man, "He a punk. You watch me, and you can do what you want to him, it don't matter."

They stood on either side of me, taking turns pushing it to my lips. Then putting it in my mouth. They pushed and pulled so hard my neck and shoulders began to hurt. After a while, they bent me over the sofa with my chest on the arm and my head hanging over.

The yellow-skin man was in my mouth, and the other man was now behind me, pushing himself into me. The more I moved around, the more it hurt. This went on for a while, with the both pushing and pulling me to them. Each time it hurt more and more.

The pain was too much. I could feel myself getting weak, feeling sick. It felt as though I was being ripped apart. He was inside me, and I was screaming, but no sounds were coming out. The man in front was now pushed all the way in my mouth. One of them would start and the other would almost stop. I tried to think past the pain. I would be alright if I could just think about something else. If I were somewhere else. It was hard, with the two of them pulling and pushing at me, to try and think past it. I could feel the warmth of the sunlight on the side of my face coming through the bedspread on the window. I closed out the sounds in my head of him pounding into me as he pushed from behind.

Finally I was going under, the sounds and the feel of them was in the distance. It must have been very hot outside because the sun felt so warm, relaxing. I could and could not feel them pushing and pulling at me after a while. I don't know how much time had passed, but later, that taste was in my mouth. He started slapping my face with himself, bringing me back to their reality. I could see and feel them once again. Their sounds that had been in the background now filled the room. When the man in my mouth had finished, he stood at the door, watching and cheering the other man on. He took out a five-dollar bill and laid it on the arm of the sofa.

"You want this money, boy?" To his buddy, he said, "I told you to stay here with me. I told you what was gonna happen when he come here. Hurry up before the others get back."

"What if he tells somebody?"

"Who he gonna tell? This is what he supposed to do for us men when he come here, ain't that right, boy? This is what you supposed to do for us. There's nobody to tell nothing to, right?" He put his hand over my entire face. "Right?" He said he was going to wait outside for the others.

"What if he yells out and someone hears him?"

"He ain't gonna yell out. Now I'm finished. You hurry up and finish." The door closed, and he begins to push harder. He took his hands off my shoulders and put them over my mouth. The smell of his hands was sickening. I could hear the other man calling to him after a while to hurry up and finish. But he kept on going. I tried to get from under him, but having him inside me and on top of me hurt. He just kept on pulling me to him and slamming into me. I hurt so much.

The room was black. I could hardly make out the surroundings. I was cold and sore and still bent over the sofa. I don't know when he stopped. In the distance, I heard a door slam. I searched around in the darkness trying to find my clothes. It had been a bright warm day. Now it was nighttime. There were no sounds in the outer room. I tried the door. It was unlocked. I cracked the door open, and the light from the living room came into the bedroom. I found my clothes on the other side of the room next to the TV. I left the room and their money.

I walked outside to the porch to see them still drinking and yelling and cursing and cheering on a fight. The man who was inside me from the back stepped up on the porch and said, "There he is, Bee. Your boy just slept the whole day away."

My father just laughed a little and said, "He just a sissy."

On the ride home, my father never said anything to me except, "You a punk and a fag." He looked at me in disgust, grunted, and talked under his breath. I now knew what was expected of me with his friends.

At home I went to the back of the house and sat on the porch. It was about two-thirty in the morning. I sat there until I could see the sun coming up. It had been hours. When was the pain going to stop? My father, drunk, and his drunk friends said I was supposed to do this for them. Why did I have to do this for them and at that place? I hated the dirt and the smell of that house and their smells of liquor and cigars and sweat and their dirty clothes and the taste of them in my mouth. It made me sick. Why was it they made me do it?

The weekend was over. Monday, I returned to school. I sat on the bench most of the time at recess and then again at lunch. The kids would come and ask to play, but I couldn't. Mrs. Miller with her curly, jet black hair and dimples looked at me as she walked across the yard to the bench, said she noticed that I was no longer having fun and that something was wrong. I assured her that I was just tired from the weekend and that I would be alright.

She said, "You don't look tired. You look sad." I didn't know what to say. I tried to tell her several times throughout the day, but I couldn't say the words. I just knew I couldn't be sad around school. I wasn't sure if something was supposed to be wrong. Was this supposed to be happening? I tried three or four times to ask David when he started. How many times had he done it? How did it taste to him? How old was he? But he looked confused and said he didn't know what I was talking about. Maybe it had not begun yet for him. He was about three months younger than I.

It was the weekend before Easter Sunday, and I had gone to the store about two miles or so from the house. My father had been looking for me and was told I was at the store. He drove up in front of the store. I saw him come in and go to the counter. He bought bottles of liquor and beer. He walked out of the store, turned to me and said, "Come on, you going with me. I told your mother I'm taking you with me. Get in the car."

I walked slow to the car, trying to think of a way to get out of it. He never said a word as he drove. Then he pulled up in front of that house. I knew what this meant. He dropped me off at the curb and left. The yellow-skinned man was waiting at his door front.

"Come on in here, I got guys waiting on you." He opened the room and walked me in. He said, "Get undressed." Then he brought two other men into the room.

This time they both took turns doing it from behind.

That evening, the horn sounded (shave and a haircut). When we got home, my father got out of the car, cursed words under his breath, and went into the house. He never said anything about leaving me there.

I started washing and ironing my own clothes. I didn't want anyone to find the blood and the smell. I always had to wipe myself off with my clothes. Even when I was clean, I would change clothes three times a day. I could smell them on me even when I had not been there. My mother's friends would say, "Maggie, you let him change his clothes three times a day," and she would say, "I don't care; he washes them his self. He can change five times a day."

I didn't tell anyone what was happening; I didn't know whether this was supposed to happen or not. The men in the room kept on saying that I was just the right age to learn to do it right. When those men came into that room, I didn't struggle with them. I let them do whatever they wanted. I didn't want to answer questions at school about why I was bruised or sore. After each time in that room, I returned to school and to the teachers and to friends and a life that was seemingly without events. No one could tell what had happened to me. If no one noticed any difference at home, no one would notice at school.

I stopped seeing Eyvonne. I turned my attention to anything that was away from home, being in ear shoot of him. After school programs, music and play-acting, dance at school became my refuge. I would ride my bike to school and Mrs. Miller would be there. She would key me to parties and theater events. She took me to meet with the theatre group that Miss Jenkins had introduced me to earlier. I had started to perform in some of the plays—small parts, one, two lines, but it was great, and the audience's applause was the warmest feeling. I longed for a day when that would be my life. I would never go home. It was what I remembered on the "Art Linkletter Show," people applauding and cheering. It was a great feeling. The other actors said that the empty theaters had ghosts. I loved the theater, empty or full of people. It felt so safe. Everyone was so supportive and always so kind.

Every so often, I would get caught by my father at home and taken back to that room. It's as though they knew he was coming. There were always men who would stop by.

The last time he happened to stop by there, the door was open to that room, and there was a man already lying naked on the bed. He was tall and thin, and his skin was very dark. He was also much younger than the others. He didn't force it like the others. He moved so slow, it was like he was not moving at all, but it still hurt when he was inside me. He also didn't stink like the others. It was the longest time I was left with one person. Usually after a little while, the yellow-skinned man would open the door and say, "Stop, you're too long, let somebody else do it." He would give them a few minutes to finish, and then he would send in the next one. I knew I couldn't do this any more. When he finished on top of me,

I picked up my clothes and walked out of the room to the front door. I pushed the screen door open and walked outside onto the front porch. I didn't care that I wasn't wearing anything. People passing by pointed at me. "That boy is naked!"

Another said, "Why would they let him out of the house like that?"

I didn't care. I sat on the step and started to dress. I watched the traffic going by and the people passing, laughing, making fun of this boy. I wasn't having fun. I seemed to be the only one they were doing this to, putting themselves in me. Sometimes I held on to the rail so tight, my hands hurt. I knew the pain that was coming, when they would push from behind.

I sat on the porch for a long time. Then I saw my father come from the house next door. Was he there all this time?

My father and five of his friends got into his car. He called for me to come and pulled me into the driver's seat. "You drive."

I could barely reach the pedals and knew nothing of steering a car. He started the car and put it into gear. He turned the wheel and stepped on the gas peddle. The men started yelling. We came so close to hitting a car as we pulled away. They were now screaming, and he was yelling at me, "Punk! Fag, you can't even drive a car."

The car went faster and faster, 35, 45, and 50 through the red lights. Every time I would let go of the wheel, he'd yell, "Put both your hands on it, punk."

The men in back were now screaming, "We're going to hit something, Bee!"

"I don't care. I have to teach this punk to drive."

We swerved around three or four cars and through the red light. I turned the car into a parking lot. He then put his leg on top of mine and his foot on the brake. The stop was so fast and hard that my head and chest went into the steering wheel. I busted my lip and got a cut over my right eye. He reaches over and opens the driver door, and then pushed me out in the street.

He yelled, "Get in the back, sissy, you can't drive."

Just then I threw up in the street. My stomach was upset; I was so sick from the smell of those men, and now the car movement had made me throw up. The ride went on for what seemed like forever as my father kept up the curse words and the threat of a whipping. He would stop the car after a while, each time dropping off his friends.

But the man kept saying, "Bee, you bring him back next time you come over, we'll teach him to be a man. We all take turns, we don't mind. You just drop him off, and we'll take care of him."

Finally the ride was over. The man got out of the car. "I'll see you later, Bee," he said as he walked away.

My father continued swearing me out. "You can't even drive, and now you all sick, throwing up. You just a fag sissy."

I lay down in the back seat. I was sore from the metal bars on the sofa scraping me. My body was sore, my mouth hurt, my head hurt, and the nausea from the taste and smells. My father drove to another house and picked up Ed.

"Did you have fun, Pete? I got three whole dollars, and Dad's going to take me to the store now."

They stopped at a store and got out. When they returned to the car, Ed threw a bag of potato chips at me and said, "I bought you something."

When we got home that evening, I knew that was the last time this would happen. From now on, I would take the backhand slap and the whippings with the electrical cord before I would go with him.

He said, "Clean my car out, your throw-up stinks."

I was sick for days and stayed home from school. He told my mother I had eaten something that one of the guys gave me and it made me sick. He said that he had told me not to eat it, and I wouldn't listen, that's why I was sick. I couldn't eat, food made me sick, I threw up everything. The school had been calling the house to check on me. When I returned to school, my teacher asked if I was okay. She said I seemed so different, so distant. I never told anyone. Whenever I went to the boys' bathroom at school, just the sound of peeing made me sick. When I go to a public restroom, even today, I can't use the toilet if other men are standing next to me. That taste and the smell didn't leave me for a long time.

Once I was at the beauty salon down the street from our house. I overheard some of the women talking about a lady who let a man put it in her from behind, and now she was with child. I kept waiting to see if I was going to be with child. I didn't learn until years later in health class, seventh grade, watching a film that the thick smelly liquid that squirted all over me and in my mouth was sperm. The transfer of it from man to woman could create babies. I asked to see the film three more times during lunch. I watched the film and listened to the explanation carefully. I was relieved to know after seeing the film that they could not make a baby with me.

I now refused to go with him, so anything I did or supposed to have done, I was beaten with an electrical cord. He would send me to get it from the kitchen drawer as part of the punishment. You would bring the weapon that was going to do the damage. You would hand him the cord then give him your hand, which he held with the grip of a vice.

But one time he took out his pocketknife and stripped back the plastic to expose more of the wire. He took my hand and with all his might, he brought down this cord. The pain ripped through me as the cord ripped through my skin. The Bible speaks of dividing bone and marrow. I thought of that as the whipping split open my skin and the more I screamed, the more he would bring down the cord. He got stronger the longer it lasted. But this one time was truly different.

Weeks earlier my mother had sat me down after one of the beatings he had given me. She told me that he was going to kill me if I kept on screaming and crying. I needed to show no feeling, no emotion when he beat me. Soon he would grow tired and stop.

"He don't beat the others as long or as much as you and when you cry out, he enjoys it, and it gives him strength to continue," she said.

I had plenty of experience with his friends, showing no feeling, no emotions. Enduring pain.

But this was pain with a capital P. If I opened my mouth and did what they wanted, they wouldn't hurt me. He was going to hurt me. As he began to crush my hand in his grip, I held on to everything that was in me. I was going to fight back with the only weapon I had, what was inside of me.

He looked at me as he crushed my hand. "So, you ain't going to cry," he said. He began to strike me with the cord. He grunted as he brought down each blow, but I did not move. I could feel my skin burning; the blood started to run from my arms onto my leg. But I just stood there. Six, seven, and eight. I counted them as he kept on swinging. Nine, ten, he let go of my hand, eleven. He looked at me and then backhanded me across the room.

I fell over a chair and hit the wall. I got up and stood there as he called me fag and sissy and punk. The pain was terrible; the blood was all over my clothes, but the backhand had revived me. I walked towards him and held out my hand, which enraged him even more. He slammed the cord on the table and yelled at the top of his voice, "GET OUT OF MY FACE, PUNK!"

He left the room. I was so hurt that I could not move. He didn't know that I stood there and did not move because I couldn't. The pain was so intense that it did not let me move. After a while, I went to my room and took off what was left of my clothes; my back, my arms were bruised and bleeding. My leg was ripped open at the thigh. I made it to the bathroom and got to the shower. The water was cool as it ran down my body, the blood ran off. You could see the wire in the skin.

It took quite a while for the soreness to go away. The bruises that were the deepest in the thigh area are still there, thirty-six years later as I write this. By the age of eight, I had learned to have no feelings, no emotions about anything in order to survive.

From that time on, when I was home I was to do all the chores. I had been cutting a lawn since I was seven, but now it was intense. There was the trash to empty. The trashcans were to be cleaned, the leaves to be picked up. The cans were to be put out on trash day and then brought in. Pick up papers front and back, clean the garage and sweep the garage. This was no big deal, but if I missed a blade of grass, I had to cut the entire lawn again, front and back, even if the blade of grass I missed was only in the front. If I missed a bubblegum wrapper, I was sent out to walk the entire yard, even if he checked it and there was none. If someone was walking by and dropped it after he had inspected it, I would have to do it again, front and back. This was part of my new punishment. When I was in trouble, he would call me in the room and backhand me across the floor. I felt nothing; I could take the backhand slaps, get up, and walk away and feel nothing. I had won the match.

It was after the Watts riots. I was now singing at private parties, which kept me busy, and Mrs. Miller felt I was safer at her home. One of the other teachers at school and a good friend of Mrs. Miller was Mrs. Silverman, a kind of round woman with light brown hair thought it would be better if I stayed at another friend of their's, Mrs. Feldman, who also had sons who were performers in the business, and she was the stage mother of all stage mothers. She and her husband had taken me to several auditions. Mrs. Feldman's sons and I hit it off in a big way, singing and dancing around the dinner table. I would go to their house after school, and most of the time I would end up staying with them over night. They were a nice Jewish couple with a family like you see on TV, everybody happy and eating at the dinner table at the same time.

Mr. Feldman was about forty plus years old; tall with dark hair, he would do impressions of Jackie Gleason from the "Honeymooners." He was a great father. He would listen to his sons working on their parts for a play or a commercial and would always give his input, usually as Ralph of the TV show. He would hug his sons and kiss them and make them feel special. It was great to watch.

Mrs. Feldman was about thirty-five, medium height, a little over weight with black curly hair and close eyes and a kind of large nose. She always wore print dresses with a belt around her waist. She had a habit of usually singing the answer to a question you would ask her, like in a musical. They loved their children, and they were great to me. Living with this family was great. They had evenings where they would dress up as different characters in movies, act out plays, and just do crazy stuff. They were fun, and they didn't care if people thought they were crazy, especially the neighbors. Other Jewish people would sing to them as they passed by. They would sing if they were asking for sugar or butter or whatever. They were just fun people.

Mrs. Feldman would introduce me around to people. She would say, "This kid's got a voice on him," but no one would listen to her. "Just let him sing." Every time she was at an audition for one of her sons, she would take me and say, "You should hear this kid sing." Soon they started listening to her. They would let me sing. Then the people hired me for their parties. Mrs. Feldman would say, "He's a small kid, and I know it looks like his own shadow would scare him, but wait till he opens his mouth."

Mrs. Feldman had us all audition for a summer season of musical productions for theater groups. I got a part in the chorus for six weeks in a production of "The King and I" in New York. Mrs. Feldman said she would take me if no one from my family could take me. Mr. Feldman called and met my mother at the market and asked if it would be okay if they did this.

"It could be a good break for him, and I wouldn't want him to miss this."

I would replace one of the other children in the show who would be away for a while. This was my first airplane ride; it took about five or six hours. Mrs. Silverman said this was a great trip for her, she would get to spend time with her sister, and the boys would get a little vacation. We stayed with her family in a large house right outside of New York. The city was busy, people everywhere moving fast, but it was a great time.

The first day at the theater, I met a tall man with no hair who was talking to the kids on the stage. He invited me over and introduced himself, "Hello, I'm Yul Brynner." He had a great voice. He spoke with a sound that made you pay attention, and he was a nice man.

I had a week of rehearsal and watching the show, then I was put into the show. Mrs. Feldman and her family saw the performance. A different member of her family each day would take me so they could see the show at no cost. It was fun being there in the city and meeting people who were called New Yorkers, but soon it was time to return to Los Angeles. Six weeks had come and gone too fast.

Chapter 6: A New Threat

I was now studying with David Hubler of the Los Angeles Music Center's Musical Theatre Workshop. The experiences I had with Miss Jenkins and her theatre group and auditioning in front of the other performers was great. I was excited and looking forward to some formal training. David was a tall, thin man in his late forties, kind of a Hoagy Carmichael look, especially when he was seated at the piano. David's workshop class was very like what is now the Actors Studio. There were always producers, directors, and actors who would stop by and speak on the arts or the business of the arts.

Jack Lemon, Walter Matheau, and Maureen Stapleton were in rehearsal for a play at the Music Center, and the class got a special visit from them. Special for me because two of my favorite actors were Jack Lemon and Walter Matheau. I didn't know or hadn't paid much attention to Maureen Stapleton's work. The class was seated in the audience of the theater from the second row back, and David was standing in the front row of seats talking to the class. He didn't even make an introduction. From the left-hand side of the stage walks Jack, Maureen in the middle, then Walter. The class just started applauding as we recognized who they were.

Jack Lemon did the introductions. They talked about the play they were doing. They talked about each other and the jokes they played on each other. Jack and Walter spoke about their work in films. One of the girls in the class gave a list of Maureen Stapleton's work. Maureen said, "Wow, did I do all of that?"

Mostly they told jokes. It wasn't quite like the other visits we'd had, all question and answer, but they did take a few questions. They explained that they were on a lunch break and couldn't stay long, but didn't want to pass up the opportunity to stop by. It was great talking with them one on one; they were so funny.

Around 4:30 that afternoon, I was leaving the theater and saw Walter and a tall, young man coming up the stairs that looked just like him. I assumed it was his son. I waved and thanked him again for stopping by the workshop. He waved and said they loved it and kept walking.

The workshop taught us how to deliver, whether it was a song or a spoken piece. David worked with us one on one on how to bring the audience in on a song or a conversation. He would say, "Although you are performing to the crowd, you are going to focus in on one person in the first few rows, and sell it to them. It will give everyone else the feeling as though you are singing or speaking to them." He was wonderful at teaching stage presence, how to keep an audience tied into every aspect of the performance.

Now it was time to learn the proper way to sing.

I had to audition for a man considered to be one of the leading vocal coaches on the West coast who only took the best. He was Irwin Windward of UCLA, a very large man with a full beard and mustache. Most importantly, he had a classically trained voice. He took one look at me and said, "You're too little to sing, and you don't have enough fat or enough muscle to control sound or air flow. Therefore, no breath control or pitch." Then he laughed his booming laugh and said, "Okay let's start."

He began to teach me how to breathe and how to pronounce words. Then pitch, note by note. Then he said, "The English language is the worst language to learn to sing properly, so I want you to learn to sing this in Italian. Then we will learn to sing in other languages." He roared with his booming laughter. "Do not worry, I'll teach you word by word, note by note, syllable by syllable."

I had made the audition, one of the few students he would accept, but I couldn't afford him. His time was very expensive. David called me a week later and told me that I would take voice classes with Irwin. Irwin thought I would be a challenge, considering most of his other students spoke several languages and had previous vocal training prior to the master class and sessions. I had no formal training up until this time, so Irwin decided not to charge me. David said he thought I had great potential, although he would never say that to me, not in those words.

A year went by, and I was singing everything in Italian. Now I had the accent. I'd spent so much time with the Feldman's, I was now part of the family. I was given a Star of David, and I could even speak a little Yiddish. Life there was so different from being at home with my family in all that violence. I was now making between $200-$400 a performance, depending on if it were a garden party or a solo in a concert, and this was three and four times a week. I was making my own money and in a big way. My mother would not miss a show. My father never came, but I didn't expect that he ever would.

After one of the shows, my mother said to me as we were leaving the dressing rooms, "Dan Daily was right, you do have a chance." We arrived home and walked in the living room where my father was sitting at the dining room table, smoking his cigar. My mother said how the people loved the way I sang and how they talked about the show in a positive way. His only observation was, "Hmm, now he can pay his own way."

I was now eleven or twelve, and I would go between the Feldman's home and my own, depending on where I was working. When I worked, I preferred to stay with the Feldman's. My family had no idea what it took to prepare. There was always chaos, constant interruptions when I was trying to learn lines or a song. My father would pass my bedroom door and grunt or mumble curse words under his breath.

It was the end of 1969; my family had just moved to a new neighborhood. We were still in Los Angeles but now at the South end. There were better schools, better neighborhoods—or so we thought. We were now in gangland, Crips and Bloods, but it was still a better house and a better neighborhood than we'd had. One night we were in the den watching TV when the news announcer said that Judy Garland had died. I had seen her once from a distance at a TV studio with Mrs. Feldman, and I yelled, "Hello, Judy Garland," and she yelled, "Hello back to you." Now she was gone. She was my favorite entertainer—a movie star, singer, she could hold an audience in the palm of her hand—everyone said so. I so wanted to see her do that, and now I never would. I used to sing her songs on the way to school every morning, "Swanee," "Over the Rainbow," and "The Man That Got Away." Later I would get a copy of her concert live at Carnegie Hall, twenty-two songs in one performance. I believed her when she said, "I'd sing them all and stay all night, and I don't ever want to go home, ever." What a night that must have been for her.

In 1970 I was thirteen and had performed at the Dorothy Chandler, The Ahmanson, and The Hollywood Bowl in the "Battle of the Bands." The musical theater workshop had been a great way of broadening the musical arenas that I would perform in. The direction I received opened doors and introduced me to people I would have never met and things I would have never accomplished.

I was away from the family home because I went from one production to the next, it was different for me. The Feldman's moved to the east coast, New Jersey, it was like truly losing family. I felt lost without them. Summer had come and gone and with that my family, I loved them so much.

I was now in Junior High School. I had met the new music instructor for the school, a man by the name of Dennis Lambert. Mr. Lambert was a tall, black man with a huge smile and a baritone voice that could rattle your cage. He was trained to sing Opera, the classics. He had an unbelievable voice. Taking classes from him was going to be very serious. He was a no-nonsense kind of guy. I had some great teachers and tutors and had met some great people in the business, but this man was to be truly my mentor and later would become my friend and personal manager. He managed the music department at Henry Clay Junior High School. He formed a new class, a voice class for soloists. He trained us vocally as well as in the business of performance: what we should know at performance, how to dress, what to say when spoken to, and our demeanor, always. Altogether this is the performance. He shared all the background information needed to survive in the business long-term. What he taught, I had heard from others in the business: "Always know your stuff, and be gracious to the audience and respectful."

School was always great for me, and this was going to be another terrific experience. I had to audition to get into this special class. He thought because I was so little that I was afraid of my own shadow. Hmm. Where had I heard that before?

For a few weeks, he auditioned for his class, but he wouldn't let me audition. I finally cornered him after school one day and asked if I could sing. I told him of my previous experience, and I said, "You don't have all the voices you're looking for, so how about letting me sing?"

He thought about it for a while and said, "Okay, no one is around, so if you mess up or get scared, it won't matter. You won't be embarrassed. What do you want to sing?"

I said, "Raindrops Keep Falling on My Head." He laughed. He began to play the introduction to the song, but I didn't start. I said, "Could we try that again?"

He raised his eyebrow at me and said, "You don't have to do this, you know."

And I said, "Yes, I do, you know." As I started to sing the song and got to the verse, he stopped playing and stood up from the piano.

"I'm so sorry. You can sing. Your voice is so big, and it's coming out of that little body!"

The voice class was full of top-notch singers, young men and women. We all introduced ourselves: there was Tony and Sharon and Oliver and Elaine, Joseph, and Ronnie—there were so many nice people to meet. Only six men and six women were to be a part of this class, and there were still voices missing. The class was to be small enough so that we could focus on performance and style.

Mr. Lambert was no push-over. He didn't tolerate anything less than professional in performance or in attitude—always consummate. Two years went by quickly, performance after performance, and regular school stuff, English, history, and math. Seventh and eighth grade and the first half of ninth grade went by without event. I had always pretty much stayed after school, usually till about 6:00, rehearsing and just spending time, never in a hurry to go home. But this was all going to change.

One day as I was leaving school, I saw a guy, maybe in his early twenties, sitting on the hood of a car. He was wearing one of those shirts with no sleeves, and he just looked rough. He seemed to be waiting like others who were picking up students. Other kids passed him, but he didn't move. When I passed him, he stood up. He was very dark and about six feet tall, lean body, but with big muscles. He had a small waist, a big chest and arms. You could see his legs were developed as they filled out his jeans. He had muscles like the guys from prison. I had visited my brothers enough at Chino Correctional Prison to recognize the body type. No guys walking the street had bodies like that, except maybe a gymnast.

I passed him, trying not to have eye contact. His eyes seemed to be following me.

"Hey, come over to the car." I stopped and turned to him. "Come over here, I want to talk to you." I walked slowly to his car. He asked me if I knew who he was, if I remembered him and did I know some of the guys at the school who were in the Crips?

I said, "No and, why would I?"

"You don't remember being in a room with me at a friend of your dad's?" I stopped walking towards him. It was him, the young dark one. He said, "I can't believe it's you. A few of my cousins and one of my nephews go here. You heard about the teacher who got hit with the bat? That was my nephew's doing." No one had reported seeing anything, but everyone talked about it. It was bad for that teacher. "Look at this." He unfolded a bag to reveal a gun. "I want you to get in the car with me, we're gonna go just around the corner. I want to show you something." My stomach started to hurt.

He opened the door and urged me in the car. I stood just inside the door, afraid to move. He stepped behind me with the front of his body pressed hard against my back. He leaned down to my neck, then to my ear and then he bit my ear. "Get in, come on, get in."

He drove a couple of blocks to a park attached to the golf course on Western Avenue, just the other side of the school. He circled around to a side where there were no cars. He parked, and with one hand holding his gun, he put his other hand on the back of my neck and put his lips to my ear. "I waited for you. They told me you were going to come back to the house, and I was going to do it to you again. But you didn't come back." He started to breathe harder. "I went into prison at seventeen and was there for three and half years. After the first few months, some guys cornered me. The first few times, I fought them, then I stopped fighting. I saw how much power they had over me, and I wanted that power. I started working out with weights. Most guys in there don't work their legs much. They don't want to have lower bodies with too round of butt, but not me. I worked every part of my body. Look at my legs, how big and hard and how they fill these jeans out. Nice and tight.

After a couple of years or so, I had size and muscle. One day they put a new kid in my cell, and that night I had power over him. I loved the feel and the power of our bodies hitting against each other. And pretty soon, when new guys came in, I did it to them too. It's better with guys because it's your power over them," he explained. "There is no power when you're with a girl, she supposed to take it. But with guys, it's always a fight to see who's gonna take it or give it. I like that. I've been out for five months, and I haven't found anyone to do it with. Until now."

I had started to shake, and my intestines were coiling up around my spine. I couldn't believe this was happening. Wasn't I through with all that? Hadn't I put it behind me?

"I hear you're a dancer or something now. My cousin told me you can open your legs and split on stage, I like that." He was biting and sucking my ear. "You know what I want you to do? These pants are starting to be too tight, I gotta let it out. I asked my Bloods to point out the one who likes to suck cock. I got lucky with it being you. I know you know how to do it." He put the gun to my legs. "You want to keep on dancing, put it in your mouth."

After a while, he relaxed the gun to the floor of the car. He talked through the ordeal, just moaning slightly in between words. He told me to go to the motel down the street from the school every Friday at 3:00 and that he would be there. He said, "I will show you real power between guys." An hour later, it was over, and he let me out of the car. He followed slowly behind me in the car as I walked from the parking lot up the side of the hill to the street. "If you don't show up, what happened to that teacher will happen to you." Then he sped away.

On Friday, gym class was sixth period, and I played racquetball. Normally I would have skipped PE and gone to the music class. At lunch one of the guys had challenged me to a game. We played hard with a good crowd cheering us on. He won the game. We took our applause and bowed to the crowd, then headed for the showers. At his locker, he said he was going to skip the shower and just go home. I undressed and headed for the showers. Four guys came into the showers, and for a while it was just their normal shower talk: who is doing it to whom, and her mother don't even care. Then it turned.

"Do you think he really likes the big ones?"

"Well, my cousin said at the park in the car, he took it big and licked it all up." Then I heard, "You better show up after school and head for the motel."

"Don't look surprised; we know about you. You like dick in your mouth. Well, you're going to get lots of that now."

I thought, "Please don't let it be all these guys too." They were all standing around me now. A door slammed and they began to whisper, "He's a fag who likes to suck big ones." They were pressing up against me and holding themselves and saying, "You want this one."

"How about this one?"

"Come on, you can suck it here, I won't tell."

One of them said, "I don't want no fag on my dick." They laughed and backed off and left the showers. They took my towel, and I stood there shaking under the water. I could hear my heart pounding and see it beating through my chest. I left the showers and walked back to my locker, wet, with them peeping around the lockers saying, "Hey, you want a towel?"

"No, he likes being wet."

"Yeah, but not with water."

I stood at the locker with them passing by, licking their lips and making sucking noises. Finally they were gone. I sat in the locker room watching the clock. It was 2:30.

I left the school at 2:45 and walked the one block to the motel. He was standing on the second floor and waved at me to come up. I walked up the stairs and entered the room. He closed the door behind me. I closed my eyes and took a deep breath. The room was quiet. It was just him, I was relieved. I'd thought it would be all of them. He explained what he was going to do. He said he was going to have me this way for a long time, and he could always find out where I was, so I should just make the best of it. "As long as you show up, I will keep my nephew and my cousins and their friends away." He had a towel around his waist and was wet from the shower. In a soft, low voice he said, "Get undressed."

I pulled my shirt over my head and then turned away from him. I sat on the edge of the bed and slowly removed my shoes and then my pants. Other than the threat of his family, there was no assault in his approach; he promised that he would not hurt me. The first hour he would guide me through what he wanted. After that he said, "You know when I did this in prison with a guy, I tried to make it hurt as much as possible, so he knew who had the power. I don't want to hurt you. I'm gonna go slow, but it's gonna hurt at first." First the initial pain, then as he continued it would subside to a dull feeling of nothingness. It wasn't the pain I remembered as a kid in that room. All I could think about was how heavy his body felt on top of me, holding me down. Three hours later, at six o'clock, he would say, "You better take a shower and get home. I'll see you here next Friday." I would pick up my clothes and go into the bathroom and close the door. I looked at my reflection in a mirror on the door. I tried to see what everybody else saw. What was it that made this happen to me? I could hear him saying, "It's just like you said. I'm gonna make him show up every Friday. You should come and do it too. Yeah, both of us at the same time. He just takes it. He don't make a sound."

I walked out of the bathroom and saw he was on the phone. Then I walked out of the motel room.

I walked the half a block back to the school. I couldn't go home. It was April, and it had started to stay light outside longer. I walked the grounds and ended up at the auditorium. The janitors were cleaning, and I asked if it would be okay if I could stay for a while. I sat on the edge of the stage thinking about the day. Something must be wrong with me, why does this happen to me? Why am I different? Maybe I was a fag, a punk, like my father said and everyone else seemed to think. All those men in that room, I did what they wanted. After a while when he dropped me off, I would go straight to that room, undress, and wait for them to do with me whatever they wanted. On stage I was something so different. I started to cry, and one of the janitors came over to me.

"One of these days you're gonna own these stages. The way you sing, you're gonna be big." He saw my tears and asked if I was okay. I assured him I was and thanked him for his compliments. I told him I was just tired from the day. I stood up on the stage and then walked the length of it. I loved being on the stage or even near it; it was safe up there. Everyone loved me; no one would hurt me on stage. I thought if I could only spend my life on stage, I would be safe. No one could get at me, and I wouldn't have to be with men in this way. Why didn't they pick someone else and leave me alone? One day I wouldn't be around for these people to get at me. There would be no friends and no school full of threats.

I left the school and walked up the hill on Western Blvd, on the opposite side of the street of the motel. I still had to pass it to get home. I wondered if he was still there. When I arrived at home about eight-thirty, I looked into the den. My father was watching TV and eating dinner. We had never spoken after that last time at his friends' and that beating. As the night went on, I began to stretch out my body. I had started taking dance, ballet and jazz, and the warm-up stretch would relax the muscles. This helped a lot to make the soreness go away quicker. I started to stretch for thirty minuets after gym class on Friday's. I thought, what if someone sees me going to this motel after school? But no one ever said anything. The guy at the front window of the motel never even looked up. There were other kids who went to this motel, families who lived there, so me being there was nothing out of the ordinary. I hoped it would not be. There was so much noise at this motel. I never made any sound. All the sounds in the room would come from him. I held on through the initial pain, and after that it was nothing.

It had been three Fridays in April and two in May. It seemed things had somehow changed. The threats were still there at school until Friday, but he would no longer be waiting for me at the top of the stairs waving me up. I would arrive and walk into the room. He'd be wet from the shower, I would undress, and it would begin, always the same. There was no talk of prison days or power. He was planning dates and events like we were old friends. "I want to see you dance, it must be something."

The next Friday was different. This time he had someone else there. I opened the door to see another guy lying across the bed in nothing but a basketball jersey and a towel. I thought I had walked into the wrong room. This guy looked familiar, but the strangeness of him being there, lying there. Where had I seen him before?

He told me, "Come in," and said he'd been waiting for me and that his cousin had told him about what we did in this room. Just then he came out of the bathroom. "He's my cousin and plays basketball at Washington High School. Ever since we were kids, we always played together. When I was in jail, I told him about what went on and he wants to do it." They took turns. It was ten o'clock when they stopped and drove me home.

Now I knew where I had seen the other guy. He played basketball in the neighborhood. I had tried never to pay too much attention to the guys around there since most of them were in gangs. I remembered him saying, "Hey, little dancer boy, you want to dance with me?" and grabbing on himself.

At school Monday through Thursday, the boys would keep up the threats and the jokes. If they caught me alone after school, they would hit me with a book or something and say, "You don't walk any different. I told you he could take the big ones. Look at the way he walks, he's a little dancer who sucks. Maybe I will be there next Friday, and he can suck mine. My cousins said they did it to him at the same time." They would all laugh. It seemed there was not going to be an end to this.

The actress, Denise Nicholas, from the TV show "Room 222" was coming to visit the campus. I was to show her around and introduce her at the assembly. Mr. Lambert's voice class was to be the entertainment, and then she would speak. The day started well, and by mid-day the police showed up to the school and arrested some of the troublemakers. The very ones who had cornered me in the shower, threatened me, and made sure I would show up on Fridays were among them. The same ones who put trash cans on fire and beat kids up after school. No one ever reported what they saw these boys doing. These boys had been involved in a hold up, and it was said that one of the older ones was killed. The news was all over the school. So for the next three days, there were no more threats from this gang of boys leading to Friday.

Friday at three, I walked up Western Avenue and as I had done for so many Fridays before. I stopped in front of the motel and looked up at the room door where he had been standing on one occasion. I stood at the parking lot entrance looking at that door. I don't know why I began to cry. Maybe I was afraid to think of how it could end, tragically or what would that take? Those guys making good on their threats? Yet here it was, over, and I was okay. I remembered him saying, "I want to see you dance." He never would.

Soon it was time for Junior High graduation; I was chosen to sing a solo a Donny Hathaway song, "He Ain't Heavy, He's My Brother." The lyrics were of caring for your brother and his burdens. I had never said anything to anyone about what I went through.

My mother had taken Mr. Lambert aside and told him to watch over me. She asked if he could be the father that I never had. It was a tall order for a young man only thirty-two years old, but Mr. Lambert was great with tall orders. He would rise to the challenge.

We spent a lot of time together. He would become father, friend, and personal manager to me throughout my life. I thought many times about telling him what happened to me as a boy and the last few months of school. All I could manage to get out was that I did not want to attend Washington High School. He knew how much I had to fend off students and their jokes, and it would be worse in high school. He told my mother that she should consider sending me to a performing arts school where I could continue without interruption. He told her that something had happened to me in the last semester, that I was different, and he couldn't reach me all the time. He said I seemed distant at times. He told her that Washington High was too violent and that I would not fit in. The students there might make fun of me and call me names.

I had another reason. There would still be that cousin from the motel who would now be a senior. That night they drove me home, they went past where he lived. It was just around the corner from our house. I had already made the mistake one night, walking home from a guitar lesson about 10:00 pm. I would go five blocks out of my way to miss

his house, but this night I took the quickest way home. He was standing out in front when he recognized me. He blocked me getting by, then took my guitar and told me if I wanted it, I would have to come and get it. He went to his garage and called for me to come and get it. I knew I couldn't go home without the guitar. I also knew what I would have to do to get it back. He reminded me of the motel and said if I wanted it back, we would have to do what we did in the motel. I hated him, just hated him. I did what he asked, took my guitar, and ran all the way home. I got home at midnight.

The thought of having to pass his house coming and going to school or to go blocks around every day for the next three years was just too much. If others at school found out, I would have to endure the jokes and possible attacks. Passing his house every day, the odds would not be in my favor. Sooner or later, I would pass that house and he would have me again. I could not attend Washington High even though I had a lot of friends there from Henry Clay. It was just too much of a risk. No one from Henry Clay knew what had happened to me. What would they think, hearing this now in high school? The neighborhood we lived in was gang territory, but for the most part, they never bothered me. One of the gang members would say to me many years later while I was visiting my mother, who lives in the same house today, "You were no threat to us. You were going to be something. So, we all looked up to you and agreed not to bother you."

Mr. Lambert took on the responsibility of finding me a school where I would be safe and where I could go on singing and focusing on the arts. I turned my attention to enjoying the summer.

In junior high, I didn't have a girlfriend until the summer vacation. I was seeing a girl named Patty Magee. Patty had attended junior high with me, but I never noticed her. One day she let her hair down and wore a dress. She was cute, cute. She and I and Sharon Chaney from voice class and Al Castro spent the entire summer playing tennis every day at six am. Al and Sharon were a couple, and I wasn't sure what Patty and I were. Our being together kind of as boyfriend and girlfriend went a long way in helping me forget the events of the past few months.

We really were the little Rascals

Graduation Day 1975 Carson High School

Hanging out with my mom, She really loved my hair...

Dennis trying to talk my mother into a tour in the south over a meal.

Mom heading to the casino.

Sammy after my Vegas open a pic I choose and he signed

Sammy At Caesars' Palace let me choose my favorite Pic in his collection of photos

February 12, 1979

presentations, inc.

dick clark

Hi Don:

If I do not make it tonight (or even if I do) please tape
your show so that I can get some idea of what you sound
like on tape.

Also, please start getting a band together for club work.

I will see you (if not tonight) tomorrow at 4 pm. Please
be sure to bring back the tape recorder and the cassette
you tape tonight. Whatever you do, do not let anything
happen to this tape recorder. It belongs to Dick Clark.

Thanks,

Peg Rogers

A note from Peggy Rogers New Personal Management with Dick Clark Productions

65

Clockwise from top-left: Opening first time in Las Vegas as a solo act Sammy Davis had pushed me to do; 1992 at the Los Angeles Wiltern Theatre; Rehearsal at the Hollywood Roosevelt 2001; 1984 at the Dorothy Chandler.

Betty L. Powers Business manager

Dennis Lambert Personal Manager from age 13 to 26

My sister Janice and Michael Curtis Bridgeforth; he later became the lead singer for the Platters in Las Vegas till his death.

Mom, Betty before the show at La'maganette SunsetStrip opening 1980

My girls Destiny and Gabrielle as Sasha graduated elementary school.

Christmas with my favorite people Gaby, Destiny, Gianni and Sasha

Gianni, my son ballet proved to help with his jumps shots he's 5'7

Domino 20 year old great dance and absolute Beauty at her photo shoot.

Domino and I at a photo shoot for the new publicity layout.

Promotional poster for the new show at Beverly Wilshire

Chapter 7: Playing the Part

At fifteen I started high school. Carson High School was a little different from any other school I had attended. To begin with, it was the first school that didn't have gates around it. Second, it had only a handful of blacks. It was predominantly everything else. It had a great music department, a prerequisite for my music permit, and an excellent theater department. Richard Schraier, a thin man in his thirties, very neat in his manner, was the music director. Anthony Ceranich, a heavy-set man, kind of like an unmade bed, was the acting and drama instructor. Mrs. Feldman had advised me to have these available together, music and theater, because people paid a lot of money for the acting and singing classes.

The tenth grade started off with my father taking me to school the first day. I don't even know how that came about. We lived about forty-five minutes by car or two hours and three buses. He decided he would take me and pick me up the first day. He drove me to school, complaining all the way as he left. "Why do you have to go to a white school anyway? There's a perfectly good school eight blocks from the house." Over and over he repeated this for forty-five minutes. He was no different from the day he dropped me off at the elementary school complaining on the first day of kindergarten. Then he told me to be on this spot at Jack in the Box across the street from the school at three o'clock for the pick up. Well, he never picked me up. At four-thirty I started walking home. It took over four hours. When I arrived at home, he just looked at me and said nothing. My mother called the bus company for the schedule.

Soon I was taking three buses and starting my day at 5:00 am. It was sometimes scary, especially when the time changed, and it was still dark in the mornings for at least another hour and a half.

In drama class were plays we were constantly auditioning for, and the spring musical was the ultimate event. Not only did I have to prove myself in the plays throughout the fall, I still had to audition for spring, and it had to be good. That year the spring musical was to be "A Funny Thing Happened on the Way to the Forum." Other than doing a benefit production of songs and choreography numbers from the "King and I" with Yul Bryner and a similar type show from the musical "Purlie," I had never done a full stage production. I had gotten quite a few solos in the choir's musical productions, and as a sophomore I had gotten a few speaking parts in the plays. Sophomores usually didn't have speaking parts.

In this musical, the chorus members played several different parts. You could be townspeople or a eunuch that did a lot of fake falls into one another or walking into walls and tripping over each other or parts of the set. You could be a soldier and be absolute perfection in a serious of salutes and marching processions. And, of course, it was a musical, so the singing was just great. I loved the show and the antics that went on. Morning, afternoon, and evening rehearsals were the standard. It was business as usual for me as I was used to working songs over and over to perfection. The long hours of rehearsal during the week as well as the weekends never bothered me. I loved it and was used to it; it kept me away from home.

My diet in high school consisted of Coca Cola and barbeque potato chips. I never took time to eat anything else except for dessert—Hostess Twinkies, which I kept a locker full of. One day I was on my way to the lunchroom when I got a message from the drama department that I was now the understudy for the part of Lycus, the buyer and seller of beautiful women's bodies. I had to be at all the rehearsals for the John, who was playing the part. He would run his lines and the staging for the scene, about five or six times, and then I'd get to run it once.

He said, "Don't worry; you won't have to play the part." It was Tuesday; by Friday I was no longer the understudy, but playing the part and had one week to learn all the lines, the blocking, and the choreography before we opened. This meant all the performers in the show I had lines with would be spending a lot of time with me. Seeing that some of the parts were played by different sets of actors on different nights, this was going to be very challenging. I spent the next week living with the other actors at their homes as their parents helped run lines with me while their child did their homework. After all, there were still other classes being taught and plenty of homework to go around, just not for me. I had been excused from all other class homework until after opening night.

The musical was a hit, packed house and standing ovations every performance. I remembered every line, all of the staging, and I even managed to get through the one song I had which was written in the key for a baritone; I'm a first tenor.

Two months later, I was in a play and had one line that I didn't get right for six performances. The drama coach and director said, "I don't understand how you managed to learn a whole musical, lines, and staging in a week, and you can't remember one line that you've been rehearsing for a month."

When my father died, I was working on the musical, "Oliver." I took a week off and then returned to find that the director had begun to re-stage some of the production numbers so that I wouldn't be out front. Some of the little antics he had given me had been omitted. He thought that I might not be up to doing them, so he took them out. I walked around in a daze. After a few days of this, he called me to meet with him.

Richard was a kind man; his father had died not too long ago, so he felt he understood what I was going through. "Donn, I know it's been hard on you, with your father dying and the funeral. I can understand you not feeling the numbers or even the show. When you're feeling it, you make the other children more exciting to watch. They pick up on all your little things. Right now you're walking the numbers. You don't have the same flair you had weeks ago in rehearsal. I'll understand if you want to leave the show, no hard feelings, you've been through a lot." He was so understanding.

"Richard, I'm not walking through the numbers because my father died. You had a good relationship with your father. I didn't. There was just too much violence in my home." He looked at me, confused. "What happened to the way the numbers were done before I left? What happened to all the little things you wanted me to do? I thought they were important to the number. You said they make the number work."

"It did, it does. I thought you wouldn't want to be out front, so I put you in the crowd. I thought you would feel more comfortable."

"I'm not comfortable, I'm bored."

"So, you're not upset about your father's death?"

"No, I'm upset about the changes in the number. I'm here to work; my personal life has nothing to do with that. With my father, you would have had to be there. I couldn't explain it any other way."

"Okay, let's go to work and change them back."

He was right about all the little things in the number. "Consider Yourself" got a standing ovation and stopped the show almost every night.

After years of drunken violence, home life was good. It was a pleasure to be home now when I wasn't working on a show. There was laughter in the house, laughter that I had only experienced at the theater or the Feldman's home. Finally our home was quiet, no explosions on the weekends.

High school had also been uneventful. School was school: a bell rings, you go from one class to another. I was still acting and singing and failing science. Managing schoolwork was getting tougher with my work schedule. I was a performer; academics were tough. My teachers were starting to demand equal time or for me to at least show up one or two days a week on time. Maybe bring an assignment or two. Most of the time, my English, history, and language arts teachers based my grades upon my reviews. Physical education was something different. Out of twenty weeks, I had been there five. I didn't need PE, I danced five or six hours a day. Ballet, jazz modern, and tap. They just ran around the yard for forty-five minutes.

It was finals and Coach Volnegle, a very large white man, ex-football looking player type, wasn't going to let me slip by without taking it. He would ask us what we thought our grade should be. I said, "An A; what else?" I was a good athlete. He laughed. He was the football coach and that to him was funny. He only knew my name because I sang the national anthem at the games, which was also part of my music permit. The fact that I sang at the games helped, but didn't make up for the other fifteen weeks that I had missed.

"No athletic scores in my book, so I can't give you a grade. You're going to have to do the final, just like everyone else. I realize it's going to be tough for someone who only stands on stage in tights and does little dances."

I said, "I could do your final, no problem." How hard could it be?

He smiled and said, "We'll see."

"Oh, White," he said, "suit up, you've got five minutes."

Thirty guys lined up in the gymnasium. As he walked the line, he got to me. "White, step out. Guys, this is White. He's been in this class since the first of the year. Now I know you don't recognize him, but he's an actor, singer, and dancer." That got a laugh. "And he thinks he's going to take you guys in the final." That, too, got a laugh. "I want you to observe his gym clothes, starched and pressed. His shirt is spotless—no rips or tears. His sneakers are clean as a new whistle. Now that's the way you're supposed to look, if you never come to class." That got a big laugh. "But we understand he's a dancer who never got his clothes dirty." He smiled. "Until today. Guys, today's final is the obstacle course. It's a timed exercise that will consist of rope climbing, push-ups, sit-ups, under hurdles, over hurdles, running bleachers, and ending with two miles, no walking."

What can I say, there were quite a few guys who passed out, but I didn't.

All through school I had been in love with two girls. Most of the time I was too busy or just didn't pay attention. There was Debbie Hill, a beautiful light-skinned black girl with dimples and jet-black hair that flowed beautifully. For a high school girl, she was built, and she had great legs. She was a color guard who was in love with a football player with no teeth in his head. Then there was Elizabeth Wallace. There were only a handful of blacks at the school, and she came in her senior year. She had brown eyes, strange eyebrows, and a wide, beautiful mouth. And she was a dancer. I was told about her by everybody since I had not met her. I had only seen her from afar and was not interested at all. My best friend, Al Castro, had been trying to set me up for years. He and I had come to the school on music permits; we lived in the same neighborhood in Los Angeles and had been together since junior high. He wanted to set me up with Liz.

"I know your taste," he would say.

"Al, have you seen the way she dresses? Overalls and a bandana? She's no Debbie Hill. That girl can dress."

Al said, "Yeah, but you're no football player."

Al Castro was Puerto Rican; he was dark—with dark hair and dark complexion. Get it, he was dark. He had perfect pitch and a perfect tenor voice and he could sing harmonies. In junior high, he had dated Sharon Chaney, a "black girl." That was not done at our junior high. Sharon had been one of Mr. Lambert's voice students. Sharon would later become my best friend, confidant, and sister. She and I would be lifelong friends, and she knew where all the bodies were buried. Well, not quite all.

Al was cool, he was one of those people who fit anywhere, anytime, and he was determined to introduce me to a girl by the name of Liz. Liz a light-skinned black girl, long, light brown hair with strange eyebrows and a big smile transferred from a school in Missouri and went right into a lead dance roll in one of our ballet productions. She wasn't in any of my classes. With our schedules being so different, we never ran into each other. Her production opened, and I had front and center seats courtesy of Al Castro, matchmaker extraordinaire. The music began and there she was, unbelievable. Her execution of every move was perfection. Her timing was flawless. She wore black with a series of scarf's. Her skin under the lights was beautiful. Her light brown hair flowed in the wind, and her figure was perfect. Debbie had great legs, but Liz had dancer's legs, and she was a goddess. She had muscle and just enough thickness and curves to make your mouth water, what can I say. I was convinced and so mesmerized by her that I almost missed the dance number.

Al said, "So, what did you think of the performance?" He laughed and slapped me on the head.

"Funny, Al, very funny. She was always so tacky-looking, what happened?"

"Well, you've only seen her from a distance."

"Yeah, I know, but she is beautiful in her true self. She's a dancer."

The show was over, and we went backstage. Al introduced us, and I proceeded to charm her, "Liz, if you look like this, why you wear those overalls and your hair in a bun? You always look so..."

Al put his hand over my mouth. "He's not always like this."

"I'm sorry, Liz. You're very talented, and you danced beautifully."

"Thank you, and you're forgiven," she said with a smile. "I hear you're supposed to be something special when it comes to singing."

I said, "Supposed to be?"

Al said, "Yeah, he's alright. Listen, we're singing with the choir in a couple of weeks, would you like to come?"

"I'd love to," she said. She turned to walk away. "I have to go. I always wanted to marry a singer! Bye!"

Al said, "Marry, did she say marry?"

After the concert, Liz and I started to see each other. She wanted me to meet her parents. Her mother, who seriously looked like Lina Horne, lived in the Hollywood Hills, was head of some hospital. The father was an everyday kind of guy. Light-skinned black man, slightly overweight with blue light colored eyes and slightly brown hair graying the temple area.

Liz and I did everything together. She would stay away from home as much as she could. We stayed out at movies and friends' homes; she didn't want to go home. I certainly could understand that from my earlier days. She was running from home, and I had done that years earlier by staying on the road.

Finally, we graduated. We had talked about different colleges and where to attend. She enrolled at Cal State Long Beach, I didn't. I spent my spare time at the campus with her as she took her classes. We still needed to be together, and I was between jobs, so I had the time to spend following her around. We were those lovebirds under the tree kissing between classes. Mr. Lambert would call me for singing jobs, but I couldn't take them. I wanted to be with her. I would choreograph dance numbers in the dance department and watch her take her dance classes; she was good.

We were both now just eighteen years old. We were about to experience life in the fast lane.

Six months later, we were married for all the wrong reasons. A year and half later, we were divorced. She walked out of the courthouse, hugged me, and walked away. I only saw her a few times after that. Our paths would not cross again.

After three months of walking around feeling sorry for myself, it was time to do something positive. I signed on with a theatre group to do a few musicals. I hoped to forget my troubles in my work. It had always helped before. I was one of the lead dancers in a troop of about twenty-five. There were some big tap numbers in the show which were going to be fun. One of the guys in the show, Cliff Mills, had been in "Good News" and was looking for a roommate to move to the beach. I lived alone, so he thought if I was willing to give up my apartment in the city and move to the beach with him, it would be great. He went on trying to convince me week after week. Finally, I gave in. Who could argue with his logic?

"You're not married anymore, the beach has girls, lots of them in bikinis, there's lots of sun. Of course you don't need a tan, but we can split the rent of a great beach house right near the sand." Who could argue?

Cliff was that boy-next-door type. You know Peter Lawford, or someone like that. ` I don't know how he thought that he would have time to play at the beach with our rehearsal schedule.

He'd say, "We'll give it the old college try," or "I'm going to keep up the British end." Whatever that meant.

For a few weeks, he tried to persuade me to go out and have girls over to the house. Cliff discovered I was a loner or at least when I was working I didn't play. The business had long been taught to me as a performer that when you're on stage, you work and give it your best, then you go home and rest so that you can work the next performance and give it your best. It's not right when people are paying to see you at your best and you're at your worst because the night before you played too much.

Cliff would say, "Jack's a dull boy." He thought it was time to have a house-warming party. I didn't even know what that meant, but he was determined.

He told me to have the bar stocked from the guy who lived two doors down, who also owned the wine and spirits store. How he met these people in such a short time was unreal. The guests started to arrive about eleven-thirty. Cliff was already feeling no pain. He had managed to invite not only everyone from the show, but the block, and I think every show that he had ever been in. The house was full of people, all types, including all his ex-relationships. He didn't care. He was determined to get me out of that mood of being alone and to start having some fun again

It was quite a night. I even managed to invite some of my old singing friends from Lambert's voice class. Sharon, whom I dated for a week and who had dated my best friend, Al Castro, was there. She'd made the mistake of bringing a date.

She said to me later that evening, "Why didn't you tell me there would be so many gorgeous men here? I would have never brought a date. There's just too many guys and so little time."

Theater people are like family when we all get together, singing, dancing and telling jokes. Running the lines from the play talking about how the audience got and did not get the jokes. That was almost in every group of people in every room. They were all over the house in every room, sitting and lying all over the furniture and on the floor. There were people in front of the house and on the beach. I recorded the music on a real to real so it played continuance for about four hours and then I would change it. A good mixture of music, rock, and pop tunes and musical number from the show albums. It was good to see so many people that we had worked with and new faces.

The party went on till the wee hours. It was about six A.M., and people were still having a great time. I walked the house, looking at all the goings-on. There was a young woman with light brown hair who passed through the kitchen. For a moment, she looked like Liz, and time had stood still. We were in our home in Palos Verdes, enjoying each other. I was following her from room to room. Sharon stopped me at the patio door, *A little too familiar, yeah, just a little.* Until then I had not drunk wine or beer or anything. Not at home, not at school. Even the thought of being drunk or even around drunks didn't appeal to me. The wine Liz and I had made us experience more than we probably would have, but still, our time together that weekend was the best, and I would not have traded it for anything. I choose a very light white wine to sip for the evening and told our guy at the bar to keep it separate for me.

By that morning, I had put away two bottles of wine, but hey, it was a party, and I didn't think much of it at that time. The run of the show was coming to an end, and I began to take long walks on the beach at night. I would leave home around midnight and return at sun-up. I didn't think anything of it at the time.

Soon I started ordering bottles of wine from Russ at the liquor store. Then I started ordering cases, and I was drinking it all. I was awake for almost two weeks, and I had not realized it. I would listen to music in the daytime, Frank Sinatra, jazz, classical, then at night I would walk on the beach. I couldn't figure out what was wrong.

Don Dipaolo, a friend from school and an actor, had come to the party, and we began hanging out together. Don had the looks of a young Paul Newman, and his talent was a close second. At the party, Don was fascinated and captivated by Sharon's beauty the entire evening. He kept asking me, "Where has she been and why didn't you introduce me before?" I would say to him, before what?

Don realized I wasn't doing well, and he decided to stay with me until I felt better about things or fell asleep. He said, "You can't keep this up, you're going to fall apart. You're always dressed so nice, and now you're a bum. What happened to you, what's wrong?" I certainly didn't know. Was I depressed about Liz? Was it the fact that the show had a short run? That never bothered me before. I couldn't figure it out, but there I was—no sleep and drinking like a fish. Don was going to help me fall asleep. I don't know how he was going to do it, but he was determined to stay up with me until I fell asleep. I was still sipping wine as the evening turned into the A.M. hours, and Don fell asleep. I thought maybe I'd take a walk. I headed for the beach. It was about 2:00 am as I walked, I thought, "God, what are your plans for me? Marriage didn't work out, I destroyed a baby, and I seem to be wandering around lost." I was sorry for the abortion and sorry for everything, but I felt like life was passing me by. Where was the happiness that should have come my way after the death of my father? I took off my boots, and I was wading into the water saying, "God, if this is what is to be…"

The water was getting higher and higher. I knew I would die that night. All the time I had lived at the beach, I'd never been in the water. At Lambert's house, at a pool party, I saw everyone diving into the swimming pool, so I did too, but I started to sink. I guess I couldn't swim. I never went to the bottom, but I wasn't on top, kind of in the middle. Tony from our voice class pulled me to the top. I knew if I walked into the ocean, I had no chance of coming out. It was cold, and my thoughts were confused. I had lived through my father and all the beatings and those men. My mind went through all of this, so rapidly. I remember Mrs. Silverman and then Mrs. Miller saying, "You're going to make it."

I don't know what happened. I remember hearing, "I gave you a gift, use the talent, use the talent I gave you." When I came out of the water, the sun was coming up. I got to the place where I had left my boots, and they were gone. Four hundred dollar boots, a small price to pay for God saving my life.

I got home and cleaned out the cabinets. All the booze went down the drain and the bottles in the trash. I called Russ and told him to cancel the account at the store, I would have no use for it. Don was still asleep. I went to my room to my bed and laid down. I woke up to Don and Cliff in the kitchen, something was burning.

I came out of my room. Don said, "See, I told you I'd stay with you till you fell asleep."

Cliff said, "Yeah, but he slept two days, what did you put in his wine?"

"Two days? I really slept for two days? I don't believe it!"

Cliff said, "Well, you did. Now what do you want to do?" He was looking at the bar, "Did you drink all the booze, what happened to it?"

"It's gone, all of it gone, and I think I called Russ and told him no more booze. No more account, I think?" Don laughed and continued to burn his food.

Two months had gone by since my water episode. I had been teaching tap classes at a local dance studio and somewhat dating the ballet instructor—well, at least sleeping with her. It was time to go back to work. Cliff came into the house one day and said, "You're going to need a new roommate. I'm getting married in a month, and I'm going to be moving out."

I congratulated him and told him maybe it was time for me to make a move. I needed a drastic change. Some of the dancers had been talking about Las Vegas. I'd been watching a TV show called "Vegas," so Las Vegas sounded good to me. I called my mother and told her I was moving to Las Vegas. I didn't have a job yet, but I would. I auditioned in Los Angeles for a production of "Guys and Dolls," a black version that was going to have a run at the Aladdin Hotel in Las Vegas.

So, off I went to Vegas. I was soon working again and thanking God. Work meant focus, and I could put all my demons behind me.

Las Vegas was full of people. There was so much going on, so many shows, so many big-name entertainers. I was meeting other dancers in shows and producers of shows. Donn Arden was at the MGM Grand with "Hallelujah Hollywood," and that show was great. I kept auditioning for it, but he kept on saying, "Donn, you're a great little dancer, but that's the problem. You're little, and everything in Las Vegas is big, bigger than life."

The hotels were big, and the lights on the billboard signs were all big. The parties in the city were big. The city was beautiful, with all these lights in the middle of the desert. If I was going to work in this town, I would have to think big. Work seemed to be everywhere, even when I wasn't looking. It was truly the place to be, and I was glad that I had decided to move there. It was my Disneyland. I met some other singer/dancers to hang out with, so the city was fun and the frolic was on. The beach and my divorce seemed years in the past. Las Vegas had become home, and the hang-out buddies were family enough. I wanted to lose myself in the heat of the desert and not look back.

Chapter 8: Vegas Vampires

In Las Vegas at the end of 1978, I moved with a couple of dancers into a three-bedroom apartment. It was fun, but it reminded me of Cliff and the beach parties. I didn't want a party lifestyle, so I moved into a furnished townhouse not far from the strip. The rent was one hundred and forty dollars a month, not bad. It had three bedrooms, two stories, and plenty of room, and I was alone. I was fine with that. I settled in and stocked up the kitchen. I had no intention of going out if I didn't have to. Living in the desert, I worried about the sun. I used to get a bloody nose if I stayed out in the sun too long. Occasionally I would lie out at the pool and work on my tan. I seemed to pick up the red tones I inherited from my mother's skin tone; it gave me an interesting look.

I loved to cook and set the table for four to six guests, even though dinner was most of the time for one, but the table looked great. The white linen and silverware on the blonde wood table was magnificent, just beautiful. Every so often, Jack and one of his dates or two or three couples would come for dinner. I'd get out the cookbook and make something marvelous. My mother taught me to prepare the meal so that when the guests arrived, the food would follow no later than twenty minutes. That would give the guests time to chat and have drinks, then it would be time to sit and dine. Then I could throw them out and get back to the solitude of it all.

The city was very beautiful at night. Other than the strip, you could look out into the desert and just see darkness. The lights on the strip were amazing. All those marquees and the names of the stars in lights everywhere. There's never been a city like it anywhere.

Las Vegas was a party town with plenty of parties; someone was always having a party. I went to a few when I first arrived, but I didn't drink, and I was a workaholic and not about to have another situation like the beach, so I stayed away from the booze. Lambert had always said, "If you're always going to the parties and drinking and abusing yourself, you won't have enough energy to work. So pass on some of the parties."

It was a great place to be a performer. The weather was hot and so was the town with plenty of work to be had. I had no trouble finding singing or dancing gigs. The first few months, I went from hotel to hotel just amazed at the size, the people, and the place-it never stopped. My schedule had been nighttime for a lot of years, and this was nighttime at its best. In Las Vegas, people in the hotels still dressed when they went out. It was evening clothes and business suits at the casinos. I had chosen suits as my choice of wardrobe on stage. I love the way a tailored suit makes you feel. When I was dancing, I'd wear a dance pant that matched the jacket so that I could move easily.

My work schedule was great, two or three shows a night depending on what the rotation was at the lounge I was playing. By two in the morning, I would be at the theatre at the MGM Grand watching a movie or hanging around the nightlife of the casinos. Either way there was no just going home or going to bed after the show. The city had too much going on for that.

I had been introduced to a couple who always showed up to the rehearsals or at my shows. They were said to be backers of shows and producers of TV and film. He was Italian-tall, dark features and very handsome. He was well-dressed and seemed to be the quieter of the two. She was a skinny blonde with big boobs, semi-attractive, and from New York. She was talkative and very animated in conversation. She would talk and he would watch you or look through you. It was a strange feeling. I tried never to stand in their presence, they made me nervous. He was nice enough, but he could look through you and smile at the same time, as though you were on the menu or something. He'd put his hands on your shoulders and massage them with no expression. Then he would smile. It was strange. They were the ones inviting everyone to different events and parties. She'd always say, "You should come, you'll have fun." I found her too pushy. The other dancers said, "She's just a New Yorker, she's really nice." She may have been, but I just didn't feel comfortable around her.

You'll Never Be Nothing

When I'd been in Vegas about a year, I was working on a solo spot and some new music for a lounge act downtown. Vernon Washington called from Hollywood. He was working in the show "Bubbling Brown Sugar," a musical at the Pantages Theater. He wanted me to choreograph some tap numbers for him since he was going to tour in nightclubs when his show closed. He would come to Las Vegas and rehearse his numbers, and we'd pal around the city. Vernon was a thin black man, five-feet ten, one hundred and thirty pounds with balding, silver hair. He was a great performer, a character actor, and dancer. He was older than I. We got along great. Vernon was also from New York, and he used to talk about "being in Los Angeles with all those TV actors and their sitcom mentalities." I would laugh; he was quite a character. When Vernon would come to town and see Mr. and Mrs. Strange hanging around the rehearsal hall, he'd say, "You better be careful of them two, they want something." So, the running joke was, "How's the Count and the Countess, sucking any blood lately?" and we'd laugh.

I was working downtown doing a fill-in at one of the clubs. One of the acts had gotten ill and couldn't go on for a few days. I got a call, about nine-thirty, from Jack, a singer-dancer, and his girlfriend who had been in "Guys and Dolls."

They were coming to meet me after my show. Jack wanted to invite me to a party. He was six-one, light-skinned with dark, wavy hair, deep dimples, and hazel eyes. He was talented. He had boyfriends as well as girlfriends, but he wasn't feminine. He'd been a good friend to me when I first arrived in town. Elsa, his girlfriend, was a sexy brunette. She was stacked with long legs, tan-medium skin, brown eyes, and she was well aware of Jack and how he could be.

Jack always had plenty to keep him busy. He would say, "Donn, you're just too cute to be this loner person, you should get out more and see the world." Jack was always making jokes.

There was usually a group of twenty or thirty dancers who partied, hung out, ate, slept, and drank together. Now we also had regular lives, like school, children, and laundry-you know, regular stuff. Jack, as usual, was pursuing me about another party. Jack would say, "This party is going to be different," or

89

"This one is a must-do, Donn, you don't want to miss this one." He'd been pushing this party for weeks, and I always turned him down.

"Big names are going to be there tonight, and it's for all the show people who don't normally get out after their shows."

I said, "You know I don't like parties. I'm a one-on-one kind of guy. I don't like crowds unless they're in the audience."

"Come on, Donn, you will love this. Live a little."

"Jack, I don't drink. Remember when I told you about the last time I drank and what happened?"

"But this is different, I'll be there to watch out for you, and there's no beach here."

I looked at him sternly, thanked him for the offer, and told him I was going to see Sammy Davis Jr.'s last show. Sammy was at Caesar's Palace, and he'd invited me to the show.

I was alone, so I was front and center at Sammy's show. Jack had said there'd be names at the party, but there were big names to see Sammy. I met the Reverend Jesse Jackson and his wife, and the faces just kept showing up. I met Altovice, Sammy's wife, and she and I hit it off (both being dancers). She was beautiful, funny, and a lot of fun. Sammy's show was everything you ever heard or read about. He wasn't an ordinary everyday superstar; he was a magnificent. He told jokes, he danced, his voice was in top form, and he was one-on-one with his audience. What a show! I was with my hero in the business that night. He simply talked to his audience like they were sitting in his living room. There was no nightclub show going on, they were in Beverly Hills at his house, sitting on the lawn, and he was just tossing the ball to them; it was great. I had seen him do "Mr. Bojangles" on TV, but when he did it live, you could get caught up in the moment of this performance, and that was unreal.

He took his final bow and left the stage. I went backstage to say hello and let him know how much I loved the show. He was so down-to-earth, as usual, just like when I auditioned at the MGM for Donn Arden. He told Donn, "What do you mean he's too little? He's bigger than me!" Sammy asked me to call him to have lunch in a few days. "But not too early, baby."

"I'd love to," I said.

Altovice said, "Yeah, not too early. He means a late lunch; maybe we can put a few pounds on you."

"I don't seem to gain weight easily, but I eat a lot." We laughed. I hugged them and said good night.

It was about one-thirty in the morning, and the city was in full swing. I decided to go to the MGM Grand's movie theater. "The Unsinkable Molly Brown," a Debbie Reynolds film, was playing. The theater had those big comfortable love seat chairs where you could act like you were laid out in your family room watching TV. I was tired, but not tired enough to go home and go to bed. It had been a big night, seeing Sammy and all. It had also gotten cold that night as it did in Las Vegas from time to time. I had on dance tights, full body wears, a thick sweater, a topcoat, and I was still cold. Maybe a few more pounds of fat would make a difference.

I was going down the escalator when I saw a dance buddy, Sonja. We'd gone out a couple of times and spent a few passionate nights together, but we were just buddies. She was blonde, blue-eyes, and five-nine with a great body and a great personality. She was the kind of person who would help all the other dancers learn an audition routine. She could pick up routines very quickly, and she could dance circles around most of them anyway. She asked me if I was going to the party everyone was talking about. I told her I was going to a movie and that I had just left Sammy's show and spent some time talking to him and Altovice. I said I wasn't tired, but I didn't want to attend the party. We talked for a few minutes, and she told me that her date had stood her up and that she didn't want to go alone. It would be a bore to walk in there unescorted. How could I turn down those beautiful blue eyes?

"Okay, you talked me into it. I'll be your date or your escort if we don't stay long." She agreed.

The house and the grounds were huge; people were everywhere. Even though it was cold, there were people in the pool and the jacuzzi in their street clothes, people outside, hanging out. This was a party. Sonja and I walked around arm in arm for a while, then she got an offer to dance, so I was alone, but not really. I saw Jack and Elsa on the floor dancing, calling me to join them. We all danced together for a few songs, then Sonja joined us.

Jack said, "How did you get him to come? You know he never goes anywhere; he hates parties and people unless they're in the audience. What did you promise him, and can I watch?"

"No, you can't," Sonja said. She laughed.

"No, you can't," I said.

We laughed and danced for a while. Jack said, "We all need a drink. I'll get us a round."

"None for me, Jack. You know me and wine don't get along."

"No, it's not wine, it's a brandy. It's nice and smooth. It won't have the same effect as wine. It'll warm you up on this cold night."

"I don't think so."

"Come on," he kept on. He wouldn't let it go. "Listen, I'll get you a small one, and you can try it out. If you don't like it, you don't have to finish it, okay?"

"Okay," I said. Jack was gone for quite a while, but we kept on dancing and having fun telling jokes and trading partners. Then Jack returned.

"I had them make yours extra light because you're a light-weight." I started to sip it. It was warm and very, very smooth. "See, I knew you would like it." He winked and smiled, and we all continued to dance again.

Sonja saw her date who had stood her up and excused herself. "I'll be back," she said, but I didn't see her as the night went on. I walked out to the pool area to watch the goings-on. I could not believe the people in the pool with their clothes on and off, it was wild. I was beginning to tire of the party, so I started to walk around. I was feeling a little tired and dizzy, but I knew it was the brandy. I went up a sweeping staircase to the library. It was quiet compared to the rest of the house, but there were people in there looking at books, talking, laughing, and kissing, some very passionately for public (in my opinion), but it was a party.

After a while, I could hardly hear them. It was as though I had been on an airplane, and my hearing was fading. I was in a cloud of confusion and nothing seemed like it was happening at the right speed. I couldn't stand any longer, so I sat down on a leather sofa. Someone was sitting next to me holding my hand, and I could see their lips moving, but I couldn't make out what they were saying. I started to lay my head back, and a woman started rubbing my face and chest. She lifted my legs onto the sofa, and then she lay on top of me with her face to mine. Her lips were on mine, and she was kissing me. I could feel her, but I couldn't. It was strange. After a while, a man came over and picked me up and took me to another room and laid me across a bed.

The room was now spinning, and I couldn't get my bearings. My head began to hurt and I felt faint. The woman who had been kissing me came into the room and began to undress me. A man came back in the room to help her. I could hear the words, but everything was moving in slow motion. She helped me take a couple of pills and laid me down.

"This will help," I thought I heard her say. I closed my eyes for a while, and the room was empty. When I opened them again, the room was going round and round. There were voices and figures of bodies. I tried to get up, but fell to the bed. I rolled over to get up, and someone pulled me back. I couldn't tell how many were in the room or now on the bed, but they were naked and having sex. The sounds were so loud. I could make out Jack's face as a blur. He was in the room. All the others, I had no idea who they were. Jack was naked, and he was now straddled over me. I could feel him biting me. I could feel hands rubbing me. I was fading, and my head hurt so much.

Jack lay on top of me, his face to mine. He was saying something about me needing this, "You need this, Donn. Donn, you need this." I could not focus my mind; I was trying to speak to him.

"I need to leave, Jack, I need to leave," I kept on saying. He would kiss me and say, "No, you don't, you're fine." His voice faded in and out, and another face would be there kissing me. The room was filled with people now, moving about, observers. Some were standing back at a distance. They were just blurs watching. Jack held something to my nose that burned when I breathed it. It sent a wave of nothingness through me. I felt so light in mind and thought, but there was tightness in my head.

For a while, it would be Jack, then the face would change. I would be alone for what seemed like a time, then I was being moved around from room to room and handed off to another and then another. She pulled me into her with her legs around my neck. I could feel her softness. It was wet. I felt as though I could not breathe, she held me so tight. I could feel, but I felt limp in my gestures, and my conversation in my head made no sense. The blurred faces and bodies moved around me and on me. I could hear their sounds of moaning. Or was it me? The sounds were so loud inside my head. The room was spinning and then

I woke up in a room that was not familiar to me. It was a large room with heavy red drapes on the windows. The bed was oversized, and the headboard was mirrored. I was in the middle of the bed. The room spun around, and my vision was blurred. I had a headache, and my body ached. I tried to sit up, but my head hurt so much that I lay back down. Where was I? Whose room was this? I couldn't figure out how I got there. There were mirrors on every wall, and I was naked. I could see marks on my neck, my chest, my stomach. My legs hurt as though I had been dancing without a warm up.

I heard the door open, and I pulled the covers on the bed over me. I looked to see if I could recognize them. I couldn't make them out, but I could hear the voice. It was a woman's, but she was blurred.

She sat down on the bed, "How are you today, Donn?" She knew my name. "I want to talk to you when you're up and around. I have a proposition for you."

"I don't even know who you people are. Where am I?"

"You are at my home. You're fine, and we will take good care of you. You're in the home where the party was the other night," she said. I was straining to make out her face. The voice was slightly familiar.

"What do you mean the party?" My head hurt so much.

"Listen," she said, "my husband enjoyed you the other night, and I want to buy you for him."

"What do you mean buy?"

"You get up, come downstairs, and we will talk about it."

Just then the door opened, and the Italian man was standing there. My vision was getting better. "And how is our dancer doing this morning?" He was wearing a bathrobe that was open with nothing under it.

"Oh, he's coming around," she said. It was the two of them, the Count and Countess. I was in their bed, their house.

"Was this your party last night?" I said.

"Last night?" He laughed. "No, that was two nights ago," he said. I couldn't understand them. They were confusing me. What did he mean two nights ago?

I asked again, "How did I get here?"

She said, "Why don't you get up, come downstairs, and we'll talk about it."

He said, "Or you can stay in bed, and I'll join you. Whatever you want to do is fine with me." That was the most I had heard him say, ever.

"Where are my clothes?"

"Just put on a robe like me, or don't wear anything. I love your little dancer's body." In the room were my boots, my coat, and a pair of someone's jeans with size thirty-two waist (I was a twenty-four). There was no shirt to be found. I got dressed and went downstairs. He was standing at the bottom of the stairs. As I got to the bottom, he put his hand on my stomach and then to my chest. "I really like your body."

I stepped back from him. "I'm not that way. I don't like men in that way."

He laughed. "Yeah, but I like you in that way."

It was the house from the party, but what happened to me?

"My husband really wants to spend more time with you. These past couples of days have been great for him. You're what he's wanted a long time. You're just right in all the right places for him. I want to buy you for him," she said.

"What do you mean buy? Like slavery?"

"No, like keep you."

She was cool and pulled me over to her and kissed me on the lips. "No, like business. You can move in here, and we'll take care of you. You'll spend your evenings and time when you're not dancing with my husband."

I turned to look at him. She continued, "He really enjoyed being with you. He stayed with you in bed these last few nights, and he really loves to see you when you're dancing."

By then all I could hear was Vernon's voice saying, "Be careful of them, I don't trust either one of them." I walked towards the door. He grabbed my hand and pulled me towards him. I stopped him.

"Don't," I said.

She said, "Think about it. It's a good deal. The car out front will take you to your home to get your things and whatever you want to bring."

I thought, *I'm not going home. I don't want these people knowing where I live.*

I told the driver to take me to the MGM. I sat in the backseat of the car and thought, what is this? Why are these two after me? I'm sure there were others who would welcome this, but I didn't need it. And what did she mean by "he enjoyed you?"

At the MGM, I went inside and waited thirty minutes till that car left. Then I went out the back door of the building. I crossed around to the front to see if I saw the car. I headed for where the taxis were parked. I got into a taxi and told the driver to take me downtown. The taxi turned off Las Vegas Blvd. We drove around in circles for an hour. Finally he said, "Are you going somewhere in particular, or do you want me to continue to drive around?" I told him to drive around; I needed to think.

I tried to remember the party and what happened, but my mind was blank. *I need to talk to Jack*, I thought, *he can clear some of this up for me*. I gave the driver Jack's address.

There was no answer to my knock at his apartment. It was four o'clock, and Jack was usually still home. It was too early for him to leave for his evening show. I got back in the taxi and went home. I called his home, called the hotel, but there was no answer. I continued to call and call, but still no answer. I went to his show at the Flamingo Hilton, and they said he was off for a week. A week? He never said he was going anywhere and that he was going to be off for a week. He would have told me. I couldn't get him on the phone, and there was no answer at his house.

For the next couple of days, I tried to get in contact, but I had no luck. In the meantime, that couple had been leaving messages around town for me. I would not return their calls, and I avoided them when I saw them around. Whatever had happened, I wasn't going to get an answer from them, and Jack was nowhere to be found. I decided to focus on my show. I was going to do a few nights at the Aladdin, and I was looking forward to the audience for some mental comfort.

I went over to Caesar's to call Sammy's suite. A man's voice answered the phone and said Sammy was not available. I left a message that I had called to schedule our lunch date and for him to call me. I sat out at the pool area at Caesar's thinking of what had happened to me. Who would believe me? There was so much free sex to be had, why rape someone? Jack was there at the party; he wouldn't let anything like that happen to me. Would he? I had no one who could even tell me what had happened. Just these two sending me letters, her wanting me for her husband. I wasn't like that, where did they get that from anyway? Just because someone was a dancer didn't mean he wanted to be with men. Some dancers were, but others weren't, and I wasn't.

My thoughts were all over the place. I was depressed; I had no answers and too many questions. I went home and laid around the house trying to think step by step of what happened at that party. Nothing was connecting in my mind. I remembered Jack and Sonja and dancing. I remembered feeling tired, but that was it. I think this was the first time I started to focus on what had happened as a child with those men and in that motel room. Was it something I was maybe doing? I hated my life off stage. It appears people looked at me so differently. When I simply walked the street, men whistled or called out to me. If I were waiting at a corner for the light to turn, guys would brush up against me in strange ways. It seemed they would go out of their way. Then they would make a remake of nonsense. I thought, why hadn't I told someone? I was close to Mrs. Miller, Mrs. Silverman and in junior high, why hadn't I told Mr. Lambert? What was the matter with me? They would have helped me. This was the first time since my break-up with Liz that I looked back at my life. What was this sex thing everybody seemed so interested in? Everybody wanted to have me, be with me that away. I hated that. Life for me was on stage. I was safe on stage.

It was about three-thirty when the phone rang, and it was Sammy calling for lunch at Caesar's. Our conversation was funny. Sammy just had a way about himself. He was so down-to-earth; you'd just never know he was a major player.

He said, "It'll just be family tomorrow." That could be a few or a crowd. I walked around the house trying to think of the fun I would have with Sammy and not about the events of the last few days. I focused on something to wear. Sammy was always so sharp, and I wanted to look nice. As usual I chose something in white.

It had been quite a lunch. Being around him and just laughing and listening to all the stories. I forgot all my problems and just enjoyed time with Sammy. I told him of the crazy party and that I woke up in these people's bed two days later. Then I told him that she wanted to buy me for her husband as a plaything to keep at their house. He said, "Be careful, this town can breed some strange people. Don't worry, you'll be fine." He reassured me as he took my hand.

He introduced me to everyone who came in. We talked as though we had known each other for years. After an hour or so, Frank Sinatra came in the restaurant. The area was closed off to the public so it was quiet.

"What's up, Sam?" He came over to the table. Sammy introduced us as he sat down.

Sammy said, "Keep an eye on this little guy, he's going places."

Mr. Sinatra said, "He's bigger than you are." He shook my hand and said, "Make sure you stay on top of all the details. You know what's best for you, they don't." He smiled. "Hey, Sam, you're in good company. I got to go." He was up and gone.

I couldn't believe that day, first Sammy, then Frank Sinatra. We talked about everything: the business and the old days, his friendship with Frank. Sammy said, "I really love that man. We hadn't spoken for a few years until dinner the other night."

We took a couple of pictures together. He gave me a picture from the show promotion. We were looking through some pictures when we ran across one of him in his earlier days. It was a picture of him sitting on a stool. "Here, I'll write a little something on it for you."

He wrote, "The Best; Sammy Davis, Jr."

It was time for him to prepare for the evening, so we hugged and said our good-byes. I left the hotel and went to the Aladdin. I got to one of the dressing rooms and cried. It was so nice being with him. He was so kind and just a regular guy. I sat there for a couple of hours just thinking of the events of the week and the lunch, but my thoughts raced with a vengeance. What had happened in those two days? That time was missing, and I wanted it back. I wanted to know. I needed to know. It had now been about six or seven weeks and still no Jack. What had happened to him? I met with three of the different girls that Jack was dating, and none of them had spoken with him.

My phone would ring, and there would be no one on the line. There would be notes waiting for me and when I opened them, there was no writing on them. It was weird, but I had a feeling who it might have been. One afternoon I answered the phone. I expected no one on the other end, but it was a man who said that he was told to watch out for me.

"Don't worry about anything. There will be someone keeping an eye on you from now on. Wherever you are, no one will hurt you again."

Where did this come from? First those people, then the notes with nothing on them. Now this phone call. What was going on? I called Vernon and told him I would come to LA for our next rehearsal. I needed a break from that guy and his wife following me around and those crazy phone calls.

When I arrived at Burbank Airport, Vernon and a friend were waiting at baggage claim. "How was the trip?" he said.

I said, "It was good, but that was no trip like the one I've been on these past few days."

Vernon said, "Let's wait until we get to the house so I can give you all of my attention. I don't want to miss a thing."

I told Vernon what had happened to me. I thought about it, whatever I had drank, that started it. I'd make sure not to accept drinks or anything given to me by anyone. I told him that Jack had left for New York and never said a word about anything; he just left.

Vernon thought my saying "You mean like slavery?" was funny, so he now had a new running joke. Rehearsing for his tour, we had completed two of his dance numbers and started the third. He could pick up the steps quick, then we would block them into the piece. We hadn't put the finishing gloss to them, but he pretty much had all the moves. Vernon's tour was to begin in Chicago before he left for Europe. I thought he should play Las Vegas. He would have been great there, and we could have palled around between our shows.

After his show closed, he was ready for his tour. We had finished the choreography and were putting on the last nuances. I decided to stay in L.A. at Vernon's for a while.

I got a job singing at a supper club on the Sunset Strip called LaMaganett's. It was totally Italian with portraits of Frank, Dean. and Sammy that hung behind the piano bar. I was in good company. It was good to be in L.A. The family could come to the shows and see me perform since it was local.

My sister Betty worked in Beverly Hills for an auto leasing company and had invited one of her clients to see my show. Her name was Peggy Rogers, and she was a personal manager with Dick Clark Productions. She was a heavy-set woman, middle-aged, but you could see she had been attractive in earlier days. We met in her office on Sunset Boulevard, down from the restaurant. She told me LaMaganett's was her favorite watering hole. It was her hang-out, so it would be easy for her to see my show. She said if she liked it, she would talk to Dick Clark about me, and I should consider putting a band together for touring clubs.

The show was a smash and the audience was great. I pulled out all the best songs, and I remembered Sammy talking to his audience as though they were in his living room, so I mimicked that approach. Peggy didn't make it to the show, but she left me a note and a tape recorder. "Make sure you tape your show and take care of this tape recorder, it belongs to Dick Clark."

I met with Peggy a few days later at her office and gave her the tape. The tape recording from the restaurant was terrible. All you could hear was the audience and me somewhat in the background. Then it didn't work properly and didn't record the second part of the show. It was a terrible machine. I said to her, "And Dick wants this machine back?"

"Yeah, sentimental value," she said.

I said, "It would have to be."

Peggy liked what she heard despite all the other sounds and said I should put together a band. After the meeting, I called Lambert to assemble a band. We set a time of three months to rehearse enough music to cover the start of a tour. The rest of the music we would pick up on the road as needed.

I had three months to kill, so I started making up for lost time. There was Yvonne and Michelle and Cassandra and Rosemary. They were nothing serious, just good, old-fashioned fun, and I needed some fun for a while. It continued all the way up until the tour, and even afterwards, I kept up the pace. I was with two girls a week, always being careful not to let it overlap into my work.

Being on tour was different. These clubs weren't like playing the lounges in Las Vegas. These were dance clubs, so I hired three girls to dance with me on stage, and we partied every night, on stage and off. It was a blast! I was still a stickler for no booze. I could party with the best of them and not have anything to drink. But the band and the drugs, the booze, and the girls didn't mix. Someone was always missing when it got close to show time. I had to call Lambert to come out and hire new band members in between club dates.

It was getting out of hand, and Lambert was losing his cool. He said, "This is not the way I taught you. You have to be responsible when you're on the road, not only for you, but for all of them. They take their cue from you, and I'm not sure you didn't start all of this with these girls." I apologized to him for being out of control. I knew it wasn't like me, but it just seemed that everyone had a great time and always at my expense.

I hadn't told him about Las Vegas, so maybe I was just looking for excuses. I cleaned up my act for the rest of the tour. Lambert had been teacher then friend, now personal manager, but now the role of personal manager would be Peggy's. Lambert would step into the position of road manager. We had been halfway through this tour, trying to get a feel for these types of shows that Peggy booked, but we still didn't have a firm deal with Peggy or Dick Clark Productions.

Lambert was not impressed with her style, he was hands on, and she was hands off. Time just kept passing with nothing solid from their side. We'd been in seventeen states, and we had four new band members. We put a clause in their contracts: no drugs and no booze on show dates. We got an offer for Japan; it would the longest flight of my life. I'd always had a fear of flying, not because I thought about an accident. I hated that feeling of not being in control. My hearing would go out, and I'd be just plain sick. Hot one minute, cold the next, sore throat, nausea. I was more than happy to set foot on solid ground.

We were there for six months playing very nice hotels and lounges, mostly in Tokyo. The city was beautiful. There were people everywhere. The musicians would joke about being on the goody-good tour and that they were in bed at a reasonable hour and sober. The clause worked, the rest of the tour was quiet. When the tour was over, I was glad and very much in a hurry to be back in the States.

A year had gone by, and I began to miss Las Vegas: the lights, the musicals, big shows with a cast of people who were like my family, those clubs with three and four shows a night and to an audience that danced the whole show-did any of them even hear me, or was I just the background filler? I knew the music was good, and the dancers were good. I'd had great training on how to mount a show, but this tour was exhausting and lonely.

I got back to L.A., and Vernon had been calling me about taking over the choreography for a new musical called "Peopets." It was good to be in a show with Vernon and a cast of performers. It was a family, and that's what I needed. The show rehearsed for six weeks and was scheduled to open at the Barnsdall Theater in Hollywood. It had a great chorus and some strong leads in the cast: Vernon Washington, Jessica Smith (whom I'd seen in Las Vegas). Jessica was an unbelievable singer-actress and had been part of a group called Hodges, Hodges and Smith. Shy Jefferson not a singer, but she was the spitting image of a poster I had seen of Dorothy Dandridge and was very good actress. The show had a good run.

I was running between club dates in Las Vegas, Seattle, San Francisco, Chicago, New Jersey, Phoenix, and Washington DC. I was enjoying the run. It was great to work every few weeks, being in a different city three nights here and four nights there. They were all beautiful cities and great nightspots to dine and meet people. I did two twenty-five minute shows. I worked with two dancers and three back-up singers and a 15-piece band, relatively small group, so the music was pretty tight.

I got a call from a man while in Seattle. He said, "We've been keeping an eye on you so you're safe, don't worry about a thing. There's going to be a bag for you when you check out. Take it to the airport and check it in with the rest of your luggage. When you arrive in L.A., don't look for it, it won't be there." He hung up. Just as he had said, when I got ready to leave the hotel, the bellman handed me another bag at the taxi and said, "Keep this one on the seat with you."

I just looked at him and said nothing. What the heck was going on? I arrived at the airport, checked in, and went to the gate. I didn't want to think about that bag or what might be in it. I just knew people were watching me, and I didn't know who they were or what it meant. I got to L.A. and went to pick up my bags, relieved to see that bag was not there. I left the airport and put it out of my mind.

Phone calls came to the hotel or my home with the same man's voice and with the same instructions every city I played. Sometimes the voice would say drive here or there and pick up this person or this bag or box and leave it someplace. This went on every few months.

One early morning, a model friend and I were leaving a photo shoot in Santa Monica, a young hooded guy came up to us and pointed a gun. "Give me everything you have," he demanded. He was shaking so much, I was afraid he would shoot us. The young lady was so shaken up, I took her back to her back to my place, she could hardly walk after he ran away. I had to carry her to the car.

She shook and cried throughout most of the night about a bracelet and pendant he'd taken that belonged to her grandmother. How could she tell her she was robbed at gun-point? She was from a small town. It was about 2:30 in the morning when I finally got her to sleep. At 7:00 am, there was a knock on the door, and a box was delivered. We had our belongings back with a note: "We are always around for you, you can count on that."

102

Chapter 9: Black Men, White Party

I had met another singer-dancer by the name of Curtis Michael Bridgeforth at the Le Parc Hotel in Hollywood. He was about my age and more singer than dancer. He wasn't technically trained as a dancer, but he could hold his own. Vocally he was a cross between Johnny Mathis and Michael Jackson. He'd come from New York and didn't have any family here. He'd come out with a show and decided to stay. Curtis always performed with a group-a duo, guy or girl. As a soloist, he was at his best. He was great when it came to holding that audience in the palm of his hand. He could walk them through all the emotions and lead them to a standing ovation of applause. If you consider the talent recording in the eighties, he was way ahead of the crowd.

We had lunch a few times and determined we were both kind of misplaced when not on stage. The show or production we were in was our home. With Curtis, everything was very relaxed. We would go to movies, hang out, have breakfast, lunch, and dinner. He was the younger brother I hadn't had with Ed. We could talk about everything, and we even kind of looked alike when my hair was shorter. We had similar body types, I was just taller. People were always saying your brother this and your brother that, which was a kick for us.

I had auditioned for the musical "Raisin," an adaptation of the play "A Raisin in the Sun." It was to open at the Aquarius Theatre in Hollywood. If I got this, I'd be home for a while. The house Curtis lived in was being torn down to make room for an apartment complex, so he had just started to look for something else when we both got the idea to share my apartment in Hollywood.

I lived in an apartment on Franklin just below the hills. It was a beautiful top floor apartment, three bedrooms, terraces, and formal dinning room. I used one of the rooms as a kind of office, and the other room had costumes in it. It could work because neither of us would be in town too often and when we were, we hung out together anyway. We made plans to move Curtis in. He really was my younger brother, and we were both in the same business. It would be great having someone around. I hadn't had a roommate since I first got to Las Vegas. In Las Vegas, Jack had been my running buddy, but we never lived together.

Curtis moved in, and we would stay up all night talking about the business. We did the grocery shopping at midnight or two or three in the morning, whenever we were both home from our club dates. Our favorite place to lunch was the Moustache Café on Melrose. I guess I didn't need a relationship. I had the stage where I was safe, and I had Curtis as my friend to pal around town. I had also told him about what happened in Las Vegas.

Curtis said that a package had arrived for me and that he had put it in our office and forgot about it. It was a box with plain paper and no name as to who might have sent it. Inside was a letter and some photos, along with a couple of videotapes. I asked Curtis, "How long has this package been here?"

He said, "I think it came last week while you were in Seattle."

The letter was in a separate folder behind the photos. As I opened the folder, I dropped the photos face down. The letter was from the couple in Las Vegas with the usual conversation insisting that I come to Las Vegas to be with them. Curtis saw the look on my face.

"Are you okay? You look funny." Just then, he bent down and picked up the photos. As he stood up, the look on his face was worse than mine.

"Curtis, what is it? What's on them?"

Curtis said, "You and others, naked." They were nude photos and nude sex scenes of me with the Italian and others and Jack. Jack was holding a glass up in a toast. The thoughts rushed through my head; Jack had been my friend, and he had been a part of this whole thing? Trying to get me to their party for weeks, he had asked me two and three times a day and every time I saw him. "Are you going? Are you going?" I hadn't put it together that he was a part of this. He had gone to New York so abruptly that I didn't give it a thought.

I was holding the photos in one hand, and in the box were the videos. I reached in to pick them up. Curtis grabbed them out of the box and said, "You don't want to see these, Donn. It's bad enough just looking at these pictures, but if you look at these and it's bad, and it will be bad, then for sure you don't want to look at these."

He took the videos to the other side of the room and put them in the cabinet. "Why don't you wait a few days before you look? It might help. You're too upset right now. Why don't we go out to dinner, my treat, or maybe to a movie or maybe a walk?" He kept talking, but I couldn't hear him. I sat down at my desk with him over my shoulder. I just sat there, staring at those pictures. I never read the rest of the letter. I dropped it in the trash can. Ten 8x10's, it was frightening. Every thought in the world went through my mind. How many others had a copy of these?

Curtis read the letter. It had said something about sending out the photos if I didn't contact them. Curtis said, "I can only imagine what's on those tapes."

I'd agreed to look at them later, but as the night went on, Curtis began pouring glasses of wine, and I was drinking them. You could tell my trust in him was great. Curtis said, "I don't think there's enough booze in the world to soften whatever's on those tapes."

I kept thinking of the night of that party. That was the only night those pictures could have been taken. I remembered how dizzy and sick I felt. Either they or Jack had put something in my drink. This must have been the plan from the beginning, to get me there and drug me so that they could do this. And Jack did it. He always made jokes about being in a threesome with just guys and how much fun that would be for him. He spoke of it so much with everyone that I never took him seriously. Everybody knew I was not that way.

I told Curtis I couldn't take it. "I have to see what's on these tapes."

Curtis said, "I better open another bottle and put on the popcorn."

I tried to put the tape in the machine, but I was too nervous, and I couldn't get it in. Curtis took the tape out of my hand and put it in. We waited. There was that room I woke up in with the mirrors and the red drapes. In the bed were nude bodies, and in the middle of them was me.

I slumped to the floor. I started to remember going upstairs, feeling sick, being carried to the room and Jack, naked, kissing me. It was all there on tape and coming back to me, but there were still holes. Curtis looked at the expression on my face and poured his glass into mine. He said, "You're awake. I thought you said you were drugged and asleep."

I had always thought whatever had happened must have happened while I was asleep. But I was awake and being moved around from person to person and position to position, with these people. I couldn't believe what I was seeing. I thought of the dreams that I'd had of this, and I thought it was just dreams, nightmares, not real.

Curtis said, "What do you think they're going to do with these?"

I lay on the floor and put the pillow over my head. There were four different little movie scenes on each of the tapes with different people, and I was in most of them. There was the Italian man with Jack and me, then there was one with just Jack and me with women and other men. I couldn't tell whether I was sick from the too much wine or from the sight of those videos. I was sick, I could feel my stomach burning, and I was light in the head.

Curtis had his mouth open, popcorn in his hand, and his glass of wine was spilling on the carpet. I got up and went to my room and closed the door. I could hear Curtis calling my name, but I couldn't answer him. He came to my door and knocked.

"Donn, are you going to be okay? I guess I shouldn't call someone, should I? Come on, Donn, answer me."

I didn't leave my room for a week and the house for two months. Curtis came into my room.

"Are you just going to lay there? You've probably lost ten pounds, which you can't afford to lose. You have to ask yourself what can you do about these tapes and these pictures? Can you take it all back? You can't, you must get up and get back to work. These people are robbing you of your life. They already took everything else they wanted, now you're going to give them the rest."

"Curtis, I don't know how many people they've showed these to and in what circles. How can I show myself to the public with these things out there?"

He said, "Well, they've been out for a while, and you didn't even know it, so get up and go back to work."

I thought of my audience and singing love songs to someone smiling back at me. I would think, has he seen those videos, or is he just enjoying the show? Or maybe while in a restaurant, people staring at me, what are they looking at? My mind was my worst enemy. I moped around and thought, *well, maybe I should go back to work.* I had heard from "Raisin," and it looked like they were going to use me as a replacement dancer. I had to forget about those people and their tapes and pictures. Who were they sending those to?

While Curtis was away for three days doing a show, he called me using a Sammy Davis impression. He was good. "I just called to cheer you up." Curtis was the first guy I had met who called himself gay. Everyone else I'd met dated girls and guys alike, but there was never a distinguishing difference. I don't think any of them had called it "gay." Who Curtis slept with didn't bother me; he was my friend and brother, and he always looked out for me. He was always looking for that perfect relationship, the person he could have a one-on-one with like the rest of the world was looking for. Except for me, I wasn't looking for anyone. Curtis seemed to know everybody in town even in the short time he'd been here. There would be different guys from time to time he'd have over to the house, and the three of us would go to dinner, to movies, or to a club dancing. He never tried to convince me of his way of life. Even if we were out, he was careful to always respect me. When we were out, if someone approached us at a table, he kept it very low-key, or he would usually run interference. From time to time, he would play mother hen and say something about this one or that one, girls and guys alike.

Curtis said, "You should meet someone nice, someone you can trust."

"Curtis, I haven't had a great deal of luck with wives and relationships. Maybe I was just always too busy working. I'm at my best when I'm working, and I don't think I have a great deal to share with anyone right now. I'm not looking, and hopefully no one will find me. I just need to work."

I had two weeks at LaMagenetts, then I was off for a week and then I was going to play ten cities back to back. I was looking forward to that. I loved to work. It had been about six or seven months, and I was back in my stride.

One night while we were having dinner, Curtis said, "I have decided that you work too much and that we should go out and have some fun. A friend of mine is having a White Party, and I already told them I was bringing a guest, so your name is on the list. You have to go, there's no reason for you to stay in this house. You never go anywhere, and that's not good for you."

As he was going on and on, I said, "Okay, I'll go," but he didn't hear because he was still trying to convince me. "I'll go!" I yelled at him.

"I heard you," he said, smiling.

I thought, *a white party and we're going to be the only blacks.* I had gone to a school that was predominantly white and mixed, so this would be okay.

Curtis said, "This one's all gay." An all gay, white party.

"Curtis, I don't know about this."

"You said you'd go."

"I know, but that was before you said okay, I'll go, I'll go, I'll go." I thought, *I could do this. It's just a party, an all gay party. An all gay white party.*

Saturday night came and Curtis was all excited. "Are you dressed yet? Come on, Donn, I want to make an entrance, but I don't want to miss anything either."

I came out of the room dressed in a black suit and tan shirt. Ever so elegant. Curtis said, "What do you have on?"

I said, "What does it look like?"

He said, "I know what it looks like, but you're in black."

"I know it's black. It's evening."

"Donn, a White Party. That means you wear white."

We arrived at the party. There was a houseful of people, all black men in white. There were no whites in the house. I had missed the point, and I began to be a little frightened. Not that they were gay, but they were black. I hadn't been around that many blacks since Junior High School, and look what happened to me there, plus these were gay black men. I tried to keep my perspective.

The house was on a hill. It was modern and high-tech with glass, metal, black carpets, and statues, and lots of white leather furniture and photographs of nude men everywhere. Curtis said, "Well, what do you think?"

"I think this might be a bit much for me, and you'd better not leave my side, not even for a moment. Curtis, I'm serious."

"You're kidding."

"NOT FOR A MINUTE."

For the first thirty minutes, he was at my side, then he disappeared. I walked around taking in all the sights, half listening to conversations, being cordial and trying to be comfortable. I felt a little like the new kid in town or, worse still, like I was on the menu. I could feel the eyes and hear the little comments. I started to think of Las Vegas. The crazy phone calls, the strange man and his wife, those photos and movies. I got a tonic and lime at the bar and made my way to an upstairs terrace where I could observe the party from a spectator's point of view. I was looking for a safe place to hide. For me it was a little out there, but it was okay. I'd been to parties where men were with men, but there were also women there (even though many times the women were with women). This was different.

I put down the glass of tonic and lime and leaned over the balcony to see the people below. There was a guy standing at the bottom of the stairs looking up at me. I tried not to notice and to not have eye contact. He seemed to be watching me and slightly smiling. As he came up the stairs, his eyes didn't leave me.

He approached me and said, "Could I get you a refill?" He picked up the glass. "What is it? Gin? Vodka?"

"No, it's tonic and lime."

"You mean no booze?"

"I'm afraid not."

He said, "This is going to be tough. Let me get you a refill."

I said, "What's going to be tough?"

"We'll talk about it when I come back." He turned and walked away, went down three or four stairs, turned to me, smiled and said, "No booze."

I thought, *okay, where is Curtis?*

It was a clear night, not too cold, and the party was in full swing, men everywhere and all that black and white. I could see him from a distance, carrying two glasses. He walked up the stairs and towards me slowly with a tremendous amount of grace and confidence. He was tall, six foot plus with a muscular build, huge hands, light skin, green eyes, brown wavy hair, well groomed. He was dressed in a white suit with a cream cotton shirt and a nice smile. He looked like a basketball player.

"My name is Cedric Thomas. Here's your drink."

"I'm Donn Everett, thank you." I just looked at the glass. No way was I going to drink something brought to me by someone at a party.

"Is something the matter with it?"

"No," I said, "I just have this thing about drinks and other people getting them. Would you mind drinking some of this first?"

He said, "You don't trust me."

"I don't know you. I had a bad experience once."

"I don't mind," he said and took a big gulp. "There." He handed the glass back to me. "Just as you requested, tonic and lime."

I didn't say anything for a moment; I could feel him watching me, smiling. I said nothing and turned to the scene below. I leaned slightly over the balcony as he continued to watch me. I looked back at him and asked, "Do you feel sleepy or anything?"

He smiled and came closer to me. In a low voice, he said, "I personally opened the bottle and poured the contents into the glass, then I poured the lime juice in the glass. I stirred it and brought it to you. No stops along the way."

I smiled. "I believe you."

"Good," he said, "now that we're past that. You're in great shape, you're dressed like a million, and you're quiet compared to the rest of this crowd. I hear you're a singer and a few other things."

"Really," I said, "Where did you hear all this?"

"Curtis, of course."

"Of course," I said.

"He told me to keep an eye on you, you know, make sure you're safe and that you might need a guard or protection."

"How nice of him. He's always watching out and protecting me in strange and unfamiliar ways."

We spent the next few hours talking small talk: news, sports, and weather. We had strolled the enormous house and the grounds and were back on the terrace. I looked at my watch. It was four-thirty in the morning and time to go.

I said, "Well, it's been great talking to you, and thanks for the protection and the drink and whatever else it is you do for Curtis."

He laughed. "You didn't need any protection. Listen, how about you having lunch with me tomorrow?"

"I'm not available tomorrow."

"How about later in the week?"

"I'm out of town this week and next week."

"How about if I call your secretary or Curtis? He would know where you are? I don't give up easily," he said.

I thought to myself, *I seem to run into people who don't give up easily.* He shook my hand and held onto it for an uncomfortable moment. I said good night and turned and walked away. As I left the house and got to my car, I saw Curtis standing outside talking to a guy with a big smile on his face.

"Are you ready to go?" I asked. Curtis wasn't paying attention to me. I said it a little louder and a voice from the upper balcony said, "If he's not ready, then you can come back inside." It was Cedric. "No, thank you, he's ready. Get into the car, Curtis."

We were on the road, and Curtis was grinning at me. "Did you have a good time?"

"I thought you weren't going to leave my side."

"I sent someone to keep an eye on you, keep you occupied. How did you like him?"

"I liked him okay." Then I had a sudden thought. "Are you trying to set me up with a guy?"

"Well, you're not dating any girls, at least right now."

"Yeah, and for a good reason. One needs to spend quality time with people. You just can't engage people in a relationship and run around the countryside. Do me a favor, NO MATCHMAKING, especially with guys."

"You know I'm not that way." (He said it at the same time I did.) We turned onto the freeway. It was quiet. The morning air was still, and he just smiled all the way home and every time our paths crossed Sunday, all day he was smiling. Monday I was leaving for a show in for San Francisco.

It was early in the morning when the phone rang. Curtis answered it.

"Donn, it's for you."

"I know it's for me. None of your friends get up until the PM hours."

He handed me the phone. "You're going to like this." He danced away singing, "Yes I can, suddenly, yes I can," a Sammy Davis song, doing an impression of Sammy's voice.

"Hello." It was Cedric. "Listen, Curtis said you're leaving for San Francisco this afternoon. What airport are you leaving from?"

I said, "Burbank."

"Great. I'll take you, and we'll have lunch."

"I don't eat before I fly, it makes me sick."

"Well, you have to get there, and I will take you."

I said, "Well, Curtis was going to drop me off and drop off my car at the shop."

"He told me he couldn't do it; he's got other obligations. I'm down the street and available."

"Okay, you drive me, but no lunch."

We got to the airport and sat down to wait for the flight to be called. "So, no foods before you fly? You do drink tonic-lime maybe before you fly?"

"I drink," I said. He ordered.

"I'll get right to the point."

"There's a point," I said.

He continued, "Curtis said you don't get out much except for your work. He said your work is safe, and you always want to be safe. You know life is a little dangerous."

"I know, I've lived the dangerous part."

"You don't seem to be offended by men who are gay."

"I'm not offended, but I'm not interested either."

"Curtis said it was going to be hard. Do you have something going on with Curtis? You live together and "

I stopped him. "We're like brothers, closer than brothers."

By then they were calling my flight (thank goodness). This was about to get strange. He stood up and picked up my case. He looked at me so deeply with those green eyes and a smile so confident.

"How about I pick you up when you return? You call me, I'll be here."

"I'll think about it. Good-bye, and thanks for the ride." I walked pass him, as I got to the door, I turn and looked over my shoulder, and he had stood there the entire time watching me as I exited through the door.

The plane took off, and my flying sickness came quickly. First the pressure in my chest, and then that feeling of my heart wanting to exchange places with my stomach. Then I felt sharp pins stabbing me in my ears. I always lost my hearing for about a half a day. Thank god the plane ride was only about an hour, and that was an hour too long. The plane landed, and I got luggage and grabbed a taxi to the hotel.

I called the house. The phone rang and rang, no Curtis. I left a message, "Curtis, no more matchmaking!" I focused on the show and tried not to think of that weekend.

The show was comfortable, an evening of love songs and conversation with the audience. This was my kind of show; the audience could reminisce of a time past and get caught up in beautiful music. The second week the closing number in the show was a rendition of the song "If" by the group Bread. A woman walked up to the stage as I was saying thank you and about to make my finale exit. She seemed to be patiently waiting her turn. Just as I turned to walk away, she reached for me, taking my hand and saying, "It was beautiful. Your choice of music, how you sing, you must have had great love as you were growing up."

I thanked her. As I got to the wings of the stage I thought, *if she only knew.* It was people like her, the audience, that's where the love came from.

I called Curtis with the flight information and thought that *was a mistake.* I arrived at the airport, and there was Cedric with a big smile.

"How was your flight?"

"Okay if you like flying."

He helped with the luggage. "I hope you're fine with me picking you up. Curtis thought it-"

I didn't hear the rest of his statement because my mind was responding, *Curtis didn't think.* He continued, "I was at your place earlier, and your home looks like a hotel. There's nothing personal, you know, things."

"Yeah, I know. I'm not into things. I like space, lots of it."

At every light we stopped at, he would turn and watch me. As I turned to him, he smiled. Finally, he said, "Do you ever get tired of people watching you, you know, like audiences?"

"No, just people in cars make me nervous."

"Curtis said you were funny."

We arrived at my apartment, and he helped again with the luggage. "I hope you don't mind, I ordered dinner. I know you don't eat before you fly, but how about afterwards? Curtis helped me set it up." *Who else?*

He walked from the kitchen, so in control, so smooth. I asked him, "You look like a basketball player or an athlete, what do you do?"

"I'm an athlete, and I'm in the military. I fly."

"You're a pilot?"

"Yes, I'm a pilot in the Air force, so I can help you with your fear of flying."

"No, you can't. You can't. I like to be in control, and when I'm on a plane, there's a lack of control. That's where my fear comes from."

"You just need to know how safe you are and then you'll be fine," he said.

"Are you stationed here or something?"

"Yes, I'm set to be here for a while. I hope for a long while, since meeting you." He had a way of smiling that told me he was very sure of himself. We had dinner, and the conversation was intellectual, about art and music. He asked me about my travels and the shows I did, and did I think I would ever slow down and stop being so busy? My life was in the business I loved; I told him I didn't think I would ever think of a time when I wouldn't enjoy being with people, audiences, and it wasn't so much busy, it just was what it was.

"Aren't you tired after your day and your flight?"

"No, I'm a night person. I seem to do my best work after the sun goes down. You should be tired though. You start early, don't you?"

"Yeah, but I'm off tomorrow. Curtis wanted me to let you know that he's not coming back tonight."

"That's nothing new with Curtis. That's why he's such a good roommate, he's never home."

"Well, what do you want to do now?" The minute I said those words, I knew that was the wrong question.

He smiled. "How would you feel about me spending the night?"

"You can spend the night."

He was smiling now. I moved to the terrace door and walked out. He followed me, "Are you sure? I don't want to rush you into anything. I like being with you, talking to you. You lead such an interesting life, being in front of hundreds of people. Does that ever bother you?"

"No, the people are great. They want you to be as good as you want to be, and they are there to help."

We talked for another hour or so. I walked to the hallway leading to my room. "Curtis's room is that one."

"I thought maybe we might-" I was shaking my head no. "You're serious, aren't you?"

"I'm serious. Good night." I walked down the hall to my room. It had been a long day. I thought, *that Curtis, that boy is something else. He's always got ideas.*

It was a warm night in Hollywood. We were on the top floor and had always kept the windows open. The terrace in the middle separated our rooms, so you could see across to the other bedroom. I heard the water running in

114

the shower and after about thirty minutes, his lights went off. I put on some light jazz and lay across my seven-foot round bed, looking at the ceiling. Before I knew it, I was asleep.

I'd begun to have this recurring dream, more like a nightmare, that someone or something is chasing me, and I'm running through this alley, up these stairs in this room with no windows, just door after door. The chase is endless and I'm having chest pains and sweating. Finally, whatever it is grabs me and just as it gets close enough for me to see, I woke up. My chest pains were excruciating, and I was in a cold sweat, it was so real.

I got out of bed and moved to a chair at the window, the music was still playing. I thought maybe I'd have some tea. I was walking back to the living room when I turned in from the hallway, and he was standing there. His eyes were so green, and his slight rugged smile carried a look of concern.

"Is something wrong?" I said.

"I heard you moving around, and I thought I'd come over and see if you were alright. You were kind of moaning."

"Thanks, but why wouldn't I be alright?"

"Well, for one thing, you're here alone in your home with a man who is attracted to you, wearing only a towel, and you don't."

"Yeah, I know what I don't."

I turned into the kitchen as I walk to the stove to put the water on, he was right behind me. I turned to back up. He was standing there, and I turned right into him. It was strange, long, a frozen moment. I couldn't tell whether the fact of what he was wearing or not wearing bothered me. Or I just couldn't tell whether it bothered me in a good or bad way. He looked great in clothes, but out of clothes he was unbelievable. Someone who evidently worked the heck out of a body, just ripped.

The music coming from my room was a jazz version of "The Man That Got Away." I gestured him to the living room. He said, "Is something wrong?"

"That's okay," I said, "it's all in the music." I sat down on a sofa, and he sat across from me on another sofa.

"You seem to have a lot going on, on the inside. You're happy, but not really. I don't know you well enough to be all in your business, but what's happened to you?" I looked at him, but said nothing. He said, "I hope you don't mind, I was over here with Curtis one night. He was upset and told me

115

of the pictures and how they had left you feeling as though you couldn't trust anyone. I don't blame you at all. How can you sleep with all that going on? How can you trust when you don't feel secure enough to? You're very special, and yet, you have no one around you who you feel special. You have audiences who love you when you're on stage, but what happens when you come off? You're alone and un-trusting of the world."

I could only look in his eyes and listen to his words. He had summed up my life in the fast lane in a few sentences. He looked at me and held out his hands. "Has any one ever just held you? Would you mind if I hold you? I promise, that is all it will be."

No one had held me, ever. No one had ever gotten close enough to. He was right about it sometimes being the loneliest when you come off stage. I could feel so loved while on stage and walk to the wings and feel empty. This man was offering to hold me. Lambert had always said, "You express all your emotions and feelings on stage, but offstage you are a walking time bomb."

He crossed over to me on the sofa and sat down. Then he lay back and pulled me to him. It didn't feel as though a person was holding me, just limbs. The wood was burning in the fireplace, and I smelled the soap from his body and felt his heart beating. Why did it feel so right to lay with my head on his chest? I could now feel him holding tightly. I remembered seeing Mr. Feldman holding his sons, laughing with them, kissing them, telling them how much he loved them and how he would always protect them. This man was holding me, and I felt safe and protected, for the first time ever.

When I awoke, the sun was bright. It was about 11:00 in the morning, and he was gone. Curtis was home and on the sofa across from me, staring. "How was it?"

"How was what?"

"You know, Cedric, the pilot. Didn't you and he?"

"I did not. What is it with you, is that the only thing on your mind? I went to sleep, and he held me."

"He held you?"

"That's all that was going to happen. He's nice. I like him."

"I knew you would."

"Yeah, but not like that." Curtis just smiled and laid back on the sofa.

Cedric called me two days later and spent the next two hours trying to convince me to go out with him. You know, just hang out together, not a date. I finally agreed, and we spent the next few weeks laughing, seeing movies, palling around, going to the theater, the Getty Museum, breakfast, lunch, and dinner. It was pleasant-no crude talk or sexual jokes like Jack always seemed to introduce into a conversation. He was just a nice guy, and the evenings always ended with a respectful hug and handshake.

One evening after returning from the Hollywood Bowl where there had been a jazz festival, he pulled into the driveway of the apartment complex, put the car in park and then very slowly, almost in slow motion, kissed me. I was so shocked. It was as though time just stopped. The look on my face must have been rude.

He said, "Was that so bad?"

I said nothing. I don't know whether I was just dumbfounded. I opened the car door, got out of the car, and went into my building. A few hours later, the phone rang. It was him.

I answered, recognized his voice and said, "No!" and hung up. I lit the fireplace and sat down with jazz going in the background. I thought about how he looked at me and seemed to watch my every move. We seemed to enjoy the same things. He was funny and serious and attentive and just a nice guy. The events of earlier that day, him kissing me. What was I thinking? Why did it seem right to me? People who cared about each other: men, women, relationships? I wasn't confused, maybe I was. I knew men who had male relationships that worked and women who had the same. What the heck was I thinking? I was getting carried away.

I thought I'd have a glass of wine and put these thoughts out of my head. The evening went on. Two glasses, then three.

The night was cool, the fireplace was going, and the music was loud. I was singing at the top of my voice when the doorbell rang. I said, "Curtis, you left your key at some guy's house again."

I opened the door, and there was Cedric. He said, "No, you said no."

Cedric wanted to push the envelope and ask me questions about if I could or would consider a relationship between two men, but I kept interrupting him. He soon realized I'd indulged in too many glasses of wine, he said. I'm going to pour myself a few of these and catch up to you. We can talk about all this later. By the way can I spend the night?

He was a permanent fixture at every show. I could see he was trying to have a conversation with me that I was avoiding. I enjoyed his company and the fact that he was very military and very respectful, but I could also see he was very into me and not just guys hanging out. Only because he was so caring and personal, and he could touch me so firmly and gently at the same time. His soft voice and manner of detail were comforting. I could look out into the audience and find him paying very close attention to my every word. He said, "I love it when you sing, but when you speak to the audience, you're so comfortable and sure. It's as if you know just what they want to hear." He begins to be able to tell when the audience was getting too close, and that comfort was now strained. He guarded our time together as though every moment counted.

Three weeks later, he'd be transferred and never get a chance to express his feelings. I went to work on my next project. Curtis moped, "You were starting to look so happy."

"I am happy, Curtis, but I was letting myself get carried away. I'm just different, okay? I liked him a lot. I just didn't know what that was leading to, and now I don't have to."

"Well now there's this party on Friday…"

"Curtis, remember, you promised, no more matchmaking!"

Curtis said, "I promised with a wink. You have to admit you two would have made a great couple."

"I don't have to admit anything."

"What if you meet some-"

"I won't be meeting anyone, and you won't be helping me meet anyone."

We were having lunch one afternoon, and the phone rang. I answered it, and it was Cedric. "I'm sorry I had to leave you so quickly. You mean the world to me. I miss you. I will be gone for a while." I listened to his soft baritone voice saying good-bye. I handed Curtis the phone. That would be the last time I would hear his voice.

Chapter 10: The Domino Effect

I was set to choreograph a production of the "Rocky Horror Show" in Hollywood and would follow that with "Bye Bye Birdie" for the Fullerton Civic Light Opera. I was back in full swing, doing one show after the next. It had been a year since Cedric, and I was glad that it ended the way it did. I think I was allowing myself to get into something like I had done with Liz. I was doing it because he wanted it, not because I wanted it. I needed to put it in its right perspective and move on, and the work helped because it kept me busy.

I'd met up with my running buddy Sharon, who was beautiful as ever. She was about 5' 3" and 105 pounds with a medium brown complexion and dark brown hair. At school, boys lined up waiting for their turn to be her boyfriend. It was always something to see her moving across the campus with them in tow, trying to be at her beck and call. She had a quiet sexy appeal as a woman, and her simple sweetness still had them standing in line waiting. When we were out, men always drooled over her, trying to get and keep her attention on the dance floor. We either played lovers on the floor, dancing romantically, or we were out to catch and danced wildly to draw attention. When I was in town, she and I were party animals. She'd have no money and throw a party at her house, and it would be packed with her guests bringing everything just to support her. They just wanted to be around her.

She was my safe date. We knew we couldn't get into any trouble with each other. We'd dated for about a week or two, with all the passion that goes with it, and determined we were better as sister and brother than as a couple. She was always either trying to set me up or to remind me of some of the girls in school with us that I never gave much attention to. For the most part, we were lifelong friends. I loved Sharon. We had a bond that was perfect in every way. We talked about everything there was. No subject was taboo. Once I took her to lunch at Musso and Frank's in Hollywood. We sat there the entire time talking about everything and nothing. I was trying to tell her about Cedric and what had happened.

Finally as we left the restaurant, I began to tell her the story. I thought she was just to the side of me as we walked down the street. When we began to cross the street, she stopped with her mouth open and was still standing in the middle, and cars were swerving around her and slamming on their brakes. I went back to get her. She grabbed me and pushed me up against the building.

"Why would you want to tell me something like that in the middle of the street? Are you crazy or out of you mind or something? All those cars almost hit me. Why didn't you tell me that while we were sitting in the restaurant?"

We got in the car and headed back to my apartment. She sat there with her mouth open. I asked her if she was going to stay like that, or was she going to say something? We walked into my apartment. Curtis was standing at the bar. Sharon said, "You're in the perfect spot, pour me a drink. You better make it two." She turned to me, "And you better tell me all the details."

Curtis laughed. "I take it you told her?"

She listened to the story, and Curtis kept filling her glass. Sharon said, "Well, Curtis has tried, and Lord knows I've tried. I guess you're doomed to be a slave to your audiences with no permanent love interest."

They both laughed and tipped their glasses. I tried to date others, but it was always with lots of drama. One woman I dated tried to stab me when I told her it was over. I was arrested outside her home when I took the knife away from her. That little affair took over two months to get thrown out of court. One young lady I was taken with, I asked to marry me. She said, "I can't marry you, you're Jewish. We would not be equally yoked."

So, there was my friend Sharon. Honest and comfortable, a real woman, and a lot of fun. A few years later, Sharon would marry one of the men who attended one of her parties, have two sons, and move to a community in Moreno Valley. Twenty plus years later, she's still married. I had my fill of dating and decided I was better off just working.

I got an offer to do a few nights at the Coconut Grove. I went by the club to check on a few details for the show.

The nightmares of long past were back with a vengeance, and then there was that fear of people watching me. I was no longer this carefree entertainer who believed he was safe if he stayed on stage. Too many things had happened. Too many people, too many nightmares. So much confusion in my mind, I didn't know what was real anymore. Those men in that room as a kid, and the man at the motel, those people in Las Vegas-it all merged together in my mind. I was spinning out of control.

I had returned from my club dates and had gotten to the point were I didn't leave the house. Curtis was gone most of the time, and I would stay up all night, afraid to go to sleep, afraid of the nightmare. Afraid that one of those times I would be having a heart attack. One night I woke in that state. I was so sick, I got into my car and drove from the Hollywood Hills, some forty-five minutes, to my sister Betty's home in Inglewood. I made it all the way there and got to her door and passed out. She took me to Daniel Freeman Hospital. They checked me out and couldn't find anything. The doctor said it's probably stress. There's nothing, no heart attack, nothing. I still told no one of anything that had happened to me over my lifetime. All that stuff was inside me. I wasn't sure what was real or what was part of those nightmares. It was something that made me pull away from the world and the audience I loved so much. I just couldn't face them.

I just couldn't. As usual, I threw myself back into work

It was a black-tie event at the Music Center and a salute from the NAACP. Lou Rawls and Diahann Carroll would perform that evening. The audience was filled with the entertainment industry, and one of the highlights was Ella Fitzgerald. I'd met her before on a couple of occasions, and she was always very positive. She'd say, "You just keep on singing, you got style."

For me, the best part of the event was meeting Diahann Carroll. I had seen her in film and on TV, but this was Diahann the entertainer, and she was great. From that time on, I wanted to sing with her. For years I'd heard comments like, "You sing so white, like Diahann Carroll." I had not even heard her sing before, but this night I had a respect and love for her vocally, with her talent and her command of the stage. She was fabulous. I thought our voices would complement each other's beautifully. From that time on, whenever I heard comments of such, I considered it the highest of compliments.

It was 1983, and Vernon Washington was executive producer of a new award show, "The Windwalkers." It was an award show that recognized other cultures in the arts and specifically the American Indian. He'd been trying to get in touch with me, but it was rare that I would answer the phone or listen to the messages on the machine. He finally came to my apartment one night about 1:30 am.

He said, "I thought I'd just take a chance and come by." We spoke for a while, and he said, "If you slow down, it will take its toll on you, never slow down. Let it chase you forever, never slow down, Donn."

He told me he was working on the show and needed me to pull myself together and go to work. Doing this show would put me behind the scenes, not in front, which was my preference. I told him I would do it. I left my apartment for the first time in a month. I know that sounds strange, but I always kept a fully stocked house. My mother trained me to be a bachelor with a well-stocked kitchen, so not leaving the house for a month wasn't a problem.

I went to the pre-meetings and got my schedule for the auditions and rehearsals. I held an open audition in Hollywood for dancers, two from each nationality, males and females. We got some of the top dancers available, but by the time the rehearsals began, I was still short one Latin female dancer. So we decided to go from studio to studio to find what I was looking for.

We were in rehearsal at a dance studio in Culver City, and there was another dance troop in the other studio working on a show for Chip Fields, mother of actress Kim Fields. There was a dancer in their troop who was Latin, so I asked if she could audition for our show. I told the choreographer the story of the search, and he said, "I've been through that before."

Her name was Domino Fernandez, Dominican, nineteen-years-old, brown-red, very thick, curly hair, caramel-color eyes, deep tan, five feet tall and a powerful dancer. She picked up the moves quickly. We needed someone with a lot of flair and attitude. She had it, but with a little too much salsa. I had to slow her down. I took her by the hips and guided her just a little slower through the routine. We offered her the job, and rehearsals got underway with a group of top-notch dancers.

Now one of the things I had always done in working on a project was to keep to myself. I never got too involved with the other performers-in this case, the dancers I worked with. I'd known choreographers and dancers that had gotten involved, and it was always a mess. I was all business.

The night of the awards was held at the Veterans Memorial building in downtown Los Angeles. It was a great night to see all the people who supported the show, especially the American Indians who received awards for work they'd done years ago. Earlier that year, I had spoken to one of the Academy board members about the selection of the choreographers used for the Oscars. They would sometimes have three to choose from, but most of the time, it seemed it had to do with who was the most popular at that time. The Windwalker's Award Show ran long, but I was pleased when Vernon called to tell me my opening number got a better review than the Academy Awards just a few weeks earlier.

A young dancer by the name of Eddie had been my assistant choreographer and lead dancer for the past few years. Eddie was a black man, about twenty-two, tall and thin, very ballet male body, great legs. He was offered and took a dance company of his own and a tour in Australia, so I needed a new assistant choreographer. I called Domino and offered her the job. She was much quicker than Eddie at learning routines, and she could remember details, which was even more important. She was always throwing her red, thick hair back out of her face as she looked on as I danced across the floor, and she would duplicate the steps.

We started spending a good deal of time together. She lived in South Gate, about an hour or so south of Hollywood. I would pick her up and drop her off since she, like most young dancers, didn't have a car. The drives were taking up too much time, so she started staying at my home on and off. We could get more accomplished this way, and I could also get her up in the middle of the night, teach her a routine, then go back to bed and sleep with a clear mind of what the dance steps were. She would remember the steps and teach them to the dancers at rehearsals. All I had to do was stage it. This way of working together was starting to be a good thing.

She had been pursuing me and was starting to fall in love. I was not. One evening we were at my home. I decided to cook dinner, but I had to run to the market. When I returned, Shy, my ex and my worst relationship ever, was sitting on the sofa talking to Domino, girl talk or whatever information she thought she could get. Domino was usually dressed in dance gear, and she was wearing a one-piece unitard in a flesh tone color. She looked almost nude, showing a great body that was muscularly defined. Shy, who was only about twenty-five-years-old, light skinned black-white mix with long, thick black hair and brown eyes. She had a great figure, very sexual in how she moved and negotiated life. She took one look at this twenty-year-old and tried to pump her for information about our relationship. Shy was an actress in every sense of the word.

You must imagine Shy, for the most part, is playing a scene-Norma Desman in "Sunset Boulevard," and Domino is this sweet young kid with an "I don't give a damn" attitude. I walk through the door, and the scene unfolds.

Shy has had one too many cocktails and as a rule, she would taxi to my apartment and spend the night, or I would drive her home. This night she is walking around the apartment as though she's walking through her blocking in a stage play. One minute she's standing at the bar pouring a drink. The next she's pushing open the doors of the terrace, going on and on about nothing. "So you're one of his lead dancers? Does he rehearse here at the apartment with just you…alone? You know when we first met, it was love at first sight. I have a daughter, and they get along just great. He's a perfect father to her. You don't have kids? No, not with that perfect little body."

I'm taking groceries out of the bags and Domino, who was laying across the sofa, is now sitting up, looking at me over her shoulder.

"His prior lead dancer, Eddie, did you know him? Tall, slim, and built brother with great legs. I think they rehearsed here too. Of course, Eddie was in love with him…"

Domino is looking at her like, "What the hell is she talking about?" with a quaint smile. By now I'm getting upset with her statements and questions.

"What are you, 19 or 20? Well, you're young."

I picked Shy up, threw her over my shoulder, and carried her to the door and down the hallway. I told Domino I would see her later. She said, "Yeah, much later, by the looks of her."

She was ranting and raving all the way to the elevator. As we got in the elevator and it started its descent, she began to laugh and pound on the door.

"How was my performance? Was I marvelous or what?"

"More like or what."

We got down to the garage. She had a convertible, and I dumped her into the front seat of it. She laughed. "How did you like that scene? I was pretty good, don't you think?"

I just looked at her and asked, "Have you had too much booze, or are you high or what?"

She said, "Maybe a few, maybe a few too many. What's going on with the two of you anyway? How about a threesome, or is she too prissy?"

I told her I would drive her home.

We arrived at her condo in the valley. She invited me in. She walked pass the living room and up the stairs. As she got to the top, she told me to pour two drinks. Shy truly was a starlet of that bygone era, and her resemblance to Dorothy Dandridge was uncanny. She was one of those women who believed in wearing very sexy undergarments, never the top of a man's pajama shirt for her. Silks and satins, and that's the way she came downstairs. After a few drinks, Shy had taken a slightly warm room and turned it into an inferno.

An hour later, we were in bed. Out of everyone I'd ever been with, she was the best. There was no one more passionate about lovemaking. Shy had no inhibitions about anything. I thought to myself, *I just came out of this relationship, and it was bad.* Shy loved the politics of show business, the Hollywood scene, and the parties. That was the part of the business I usually liked to avoid. I wasn't looking to be back in that relationship.

It was about 11 am the next morning. I was coming up to her bedroom from the kitchen with a tray, toast, coffee, and orange juice. Shy was finishing a call. I said, "You know, your little performance last night with Domino had no impact on her at all. She's truly a free spirit." I sipped the juice and handed the glass. "See you next time."

She smiled. "Bye."

Domino and I continued to date and and about a year later, Domino and I were to attend the premier at Mann's Chinese Theater in Hollywood of the comedy film, "I'm Gonna Get You Sucker." Just as we were about to enter the theater, Shy was standing at the entrance.

"Well, we're a threesome again…"

She would later refer to Domino as the home-wrecker whenever we or I saw her around town.

Domino and I worked and danced and played together. She would take me to house parties in the ghetto that were out of control. I had never been to house parties like these. They were young kids and wild, not like Las Vegas wild, but ghetto wild. She was wild and when we came home from the party, there was passion all over the house. We were dancers, and our bodies in motion were the ballet. Being with her was an adventure. There was nothing conservative about her. I mean that in a good way.

She had a vulnerable woman-child quality with an explosive sensuality, and the free spirit of a gypsy. We would often drive to Malibu, spend the night at the beach, spend all day at the water working on our tans, have lunch, then dinner, then make love under the stars. One evening when we were at the beach, we made love in a convertible. We saw the police shining their lights on other cars. We got on the road down Pacific Coast Highway, as she was telling me, "You've got to put your pants on before we get pulled over." I was driving and getting dressed. We set a new world record.

We were gypsies, and off into the night we went. We would leave rehearsal and go to the beach; the house in Hollywood was vacant for almost the entire summer. She was fun and different from other girls I'd dated. They loved being around show business. She was happy being home when we weren't working. She was quiet and when we were home, she would read books, lots of books, two and three a day. I would listen to music and watch old movies. Sometimes the TV would be on, and the music would be going. Sometimes that's how I got my best ideas for dance segments.

Everywhere we went, people seemed to asking me if we were married. By now, my sister Betty had gotten into the act with, "You should settle down. All your old friends are married and have families."

This went on for about a year. By now Domino and I had pretty much gone our separate ways. One evening she told me, "When you figure out what the fuck you want, call me."

Occasionally we would run into each other at a club. I would call her for weeks and could not catch up with her, and this was starting to bother me. I was starting to miss her, and Betty did not let up. She'd say, "This girl is perfect for you, she does the same things you do. She will take a bus to meet you at church. What other girls are you seeing who will do that?"

I guess she was starting to make sense. So, I started to pursue Domino.

This was easier said than done. She was never home. I would only see her out at clubs with dates. I wasn't jealous, I was just tired of chasing her down. Every time I called her home, I spoke to her brother, her sister, her brother, her sister-she was never there. Finally when I caught up to her, she had been a model in a hair show. They had cut her hair into this punked out style. I told her to call me when her hair grew out.

About six months later, New Year's Eve, we had a date. Of course, her hair had grown out. She had such a long, thick mane that it was a sin to cut her beautiful thick curls. You know these hair stylists, they're cut-crazy. Just as we began to get serious, her mother stepped in. Her mother came to the Hollywood apartment to talk to us, and specifically her daughter, about how serious we were. Her mother was a woman who read cards and did healings. She was considered a white witch; that was one of the reasons why I never was invited into Domino's home. When I would drive her home, she was never sure if her mother would have a house full of people waiting to be healed or have the cards read.

Her mother was concerned that her daughter was serious about marrying someone, as she said, who had a dark cloud over his head. Maybe it was some of the people I had known in Las Vegas, or maybe it was my recurring nightmare. I didn't know what to make of her feelings, but they were hers, and they were not going to interfere with me marrying her daughter. Her mother was not on my side. She felt that because of me, her daughter would go through a lot of pain.

That day in the apartment she said to me, "You better take care of her. I did not bring her into this world to suffer."

I had so much baggage from years past. I had never spoken to anyone about it. It wasn't that it was a secret, it's just that there was so much pain, I didn't know where to begin. Her mother was right, there were dark clouds, some darker than others. I didn't want to scare her before we married. So I got one of the tapes of what happened to me in Las Vegas from Curtis. I wanted to show her the tape. I didn't want any surprises later if something came up (and things seem to have a way of coming up). If she didn't want to be with me after she had seen it, there would be no hard feelings. I knew I wouldn't be able it to explain to her in a way that would make sense. It still didn't make sense to me.

Well, I was out one day, and she was looking for a tape to put on, and that was one of the tapes in the stack. She was watching it when I walked in. It still shocked and appalled me to see it. I couldn't have imagined what she was thinking as I looked at her face. She was calm as her eyes watched the screen. She took the tape out and turned around and there I was, standing there. I told her that I had gotten the tape so she could see it and that I was sorry that it was left it in plain sight. I told her that I was not in the habit, in spite of how it looked, of making pornography films. It was made without my knowledge or approval.

None of what I was saying made sense to her or me. I explained to her that I couldn't explain the tape or what went on in the tape, it just was what it was or wasn't. I felt the hurt of it all over again. Seeing the tape brought the feelings rushing back, there was nothing I could do then and there wasn't anything now. As we talked about it, she wasn't blown away by the sex. She was upset with the way I was being kissed in the film. She thought it showed passion, and that was upsetting to her. But I never fully explained how I got into that situation, I thought going into it would mean going into my whole life, and there were things in my life I didn't understand.

We decided to marry in my favorite town, Las Vegas, despite what had happened to me there a few years earlier. It was going to be great showing her all the spots I had worked at. The hotels and the clubs. She loved the hotels-the Aladdin, the Hilton, and of course, where we stayed, the MGM.

We missed three flights waiting for her mother to bring the dress to the airport. I thought she was doing this on purpose, maybe to hopefully delay the marriage. As I soon learned, she was late to everything.

The city was beautiful, as usual. For me, it had a feeling of home. I loved walking Domino through the lobby of the MGM, onto the elevator, and to our room as I carried over the threshold. We arrived on October 4th, 1984 and planned to be married the next day at one of the little wedding chapels.

That first night, we would see a couple of shows. We were center stage at the MGM and then off to Caesar's. Gliding across that escalator, looking out at all the lights, it was beautiful. I wished that Sammy was in town that week. That would have been the icing on the cake.

We walked through the casino and out to the pool area. We shot photos of her lying across the concrete walls next to the statues. As we danced around the pool, people were starting to gather around to watch. The crowd got bigger and bigger. We were in full swing, doing a salsa, as I lifted her into a triple jazz turn. As she landed, we were hand in hand. They began to applaude and cheer. Two dancers doing what we did best.

They were around us and asking us if we were in the show tonight. We laughed and thanked them. We told them we were in town to get married tomorrow. We danced in the lobby and out the door onto the street, just having fun.

The next day, we continued our tour of the city and the MGM. She laughed and thought it was so funny how people would line up to get into the cage and pose with a man-eating lion.

The limousine arrived to pick us up, and we were dressed in wedding attire. In Las Vegas, people have been known to get married in whatever they were wearing last. It was great to see so many people there, getting married. Besides, how many other couples could say they had Elvis at their wedding?

We were off to a good start, being married and working on projects. I always worked a danced step in my head over and over if I were in bed and something came to mind. I wouldn't be able to sleep until I worked out all the details of a move. So I would get her out of bed and work the step on her. Once she had it, I could get it off my mind. I could get her up in the middle of the night, put a dance step on her, and go back to bed. It was legal, she was my wife. I could go back to sleep with a clear conscience. Eddie, my old assistant, I always had to call him on the phone. I would have to give him the counts, he'd write them down on something. Usually he would forget to bring whatever he wrote it down on to rehearsal. So, it would be lost, and I still would not have gotten any sleep.

We worked on show after show. Our ability to think alike about dance moves was in tune. She knew exactly when I wanted a movement in a sequence of steps.

Our working together was great, but just regular home life became challenging. I had so much baggage that I had brought into our marriage. I never talked to anyone about my past, including her. The fact that I didn't have great feelings toward anything made our marriage harder than it needed to be. My past life would begin to haunt me, dark clouds maybe. I always loved her, but I had no real way of showing her. Her small family was so close, so loving, and mine so large and so UN-loving. We had so much hurt that we couldn't find visible love; we were all behind protective walls.

The lack of emotion was starting to get to Domino. She had always been so full of love and craved to be loved. I would always say, "Don't you change. I need to be more like you." That was easier said than done. The damage from my earlier life had taken its toll, but I didn't know how much.

By now the phone calls were coming every so often with basically the same instructions. Pick this up, drop this off. I never saw anyone or gave whatever they left me to anyone, just locations. The caller said, "We'll watch out for you, and you do these little things for us."

I was still having nightmares, the same dream, and I'd wake up with chest pains and soaked. Domino couldn't understand my problems. All she knew was that whatever I wasn't saying was destroying her. We'd been married now for one year when we delivered our little girl Gabrielle. Domino went into labor about eight o'clock that evening, and we went to the hospital about eleven-thirty. What we didn't know was that she was going to have to deliver by cesarean section. So she pushed all night long until about six thirty AM the next morning, then they informed her of the knife.

Hospitals had always made me sick, so I couldn't be her coach. I spent most of the time walking to the nearest exit out of the hospital. The smell of whatever that was made me sick, like I was going to pass out.

Gabrielle was born December 28th, 1986 and weighed six pounds. She had a little pointed head, all that pushing and the walls being too small, and she was white as a ghost, like Casper. We called her Papa Smurf. Gabrielle brought a lot of happiness, at least to me. She would wake every two hours to eat. I would feed her; she was on my nighttime schedule, so it didn't bother me. She would drink a few sips and fall asleep lying on my chest. I loved it. Gabrielle brought great peace to me when I didn't understand why I couldn't be at peace.

The decision to leave the business was weighing on my heart. Domino was still not happy. She didn't feel loved, and adding Gabrielle to our family didn't bring more love her way. We went on with our little family. We had decided to move out of Hollywood and out to the San Fernando Valley. It was time to slow down on the projects and focus on the family. That decision would add considerably to our problems. It meant less money for one thing, which I don't think either one of us had thought about. It would be a drastic change in our life and in what had made our life together so right. Our creative talents would be put on the back burner. God had given us gifts to use, to give life to us and to others, and we were starting to close the door on those gifts. At that time, we had no idea of the devastation the lack of creativity would do. Moving to the valley did nothing to help our marriage.

Gabrielle started to walk, and we decided to find regular jobs. We didn't want to be running around the countryside. Domino went to work for a law firm in downtown LA, and I went to work for a computer training school. It was different, but I knew it was going to be hard and that I would have to spend a great deal of time at the job just getting to know what I was doing. The nights got later, and Domino was alone. It was just she and Gabrielle, and she was feeling unloved. I didn't know why we were so unhappy, why she was so unhappy. I tried to be more loving to her. More of what she wanted and needed, but it wasn't enough. She was miserable in our marriage. I was just floating through space.

I was so busy not knowing what I was doing that I never noticed that she was gone. Not physically, but mind and spirit, and her love was gone to someone she had met. Domino had always been a great lover of poetry. She read it, she wrote it, it was a part of her. So her meeting someone who was a poet was special. Their relationship consisted of love and poetry.

In our home, the bills were mounting. As a performer, I'd always had enough money from one project to the next. The money I made from this job didn't pay at all what I had been used to. I wasn't all over the country or out of the country. I was working crazy hours trying to be something I was not, a salesman. It was hard work. We were together, so I thought. She was happy with him, and I believe she was in love with him. We had problems at home and, with him, she could live in his world of poetry and lovemaking. She could feel whole again, loved and in love.

It went on for a while, and it's not that she wasn't discreet. The people who had watched over me since leaving Las Vegas after those pictures and videos came out were to make sure nothing like that ever happened again. They now kept an eye on my little family. I got a call that said Domino was meeting someone, kissing him at his door and having what appeared to be an affair. At first I was very upset. We had made this decision to change our lives, and now she was elsewhere, and I was living in this new nightmare.

One evening I was working, and she'd told me she and Gabrielle would be at her friend's home, but I called to see if they had made it to the house. They had not, so I called every hour for four hours. Where were they? Had something happened? I called the Highway Patrol and put them on alert to look for her car. I called her friend's home where she had said she would be, and there was no answer. Finally after several attempts all night to get her on the phone, she answered the phone. Her reason for missing was so ridiculous that I pressed the issue and told her of what I knew. Then she owned up to it. I went home to talk it out with her. I had her call him on the phone to tell him it was over. I threatened to have him hurt by the very people who were protecting me. She told him it was over and that she didn't want him hurt because of her. From that day on, she feared me, and I knew that I had ruined her happiness. She was in love with this man, and I had destroyed this. I couldn't give her what she needed, but she and Gabrielle were my family. I didn't want to give them up. From that time on, our relationship would be different.

I went back to a sales job I hated. I thought I should be able to do this. It's just like being on stage, you must sell yourself to the audience, get their approval, and this was no different. Whatever the product is, they still must like you first. Whoever bought anything from someone they didn't like?

It was the top of the nineties, and Domino and I had managed to stay together. She was now pregnant with our second child, Destiny. Domino delivered Destiny, whom I thought was going to be a boy. I could have sworn that the doctor said the test showed it to be a boy. It was another girl, and this time I was in the delivery room. Domino had her second caesarean section. There was a tent, if you will, that covered Domino just below the breast area which was the side the doctors and nurses were on, and I was above the tent. They started this process of delivery and all I could feel holding Domino's hand was that the table she was on was being pulled and rocked as they were having a tough time taking the baby out of her. It was quite something to see. Later the doctor would say, with all her muscle from all those sit ups, we had quite a time separating that muscle after we cut her open. For me that was too much information.

There was Destiny, born in Santa Monica Hospital. She was different from Gabrielle. She never cried. Gabrielle was so small that she never ate enough to fill her up, so she'd wake up every two hours. Destiny ate a lot and slept and slept. You'd have to put a mirror to her nose to see if she was breathing. One time she didn't get enough to eat and was so upset that she stopped breathing and turned blue. I had to give her mouth to mouth, and the doctor said to take her into hot steam to make her perspire so she would breathe on her own. It worked, and she was fine.

The company I worked for went through a merger, and I lost the job. This was a tough time, with a wife, two children and for the first time in my working life, nothing in the wings to fall back on. It put a bigger strain on a marriage that didn't need any more strain. Domino continued to go through the motions of marriage, and I continued to be lost in our marriage. We were both going through the motions, and it wasn't getting any easier.

During this time, I heard that Sammy was sick. It had been ten years since we sat at lunch talking and laughing. Although we had spent time together on other occasions and would see each other from time to time, my mind was back at Caesar's in the late seventies with Sammy and Frank. I called his house, but couldn't get him on the phone. I heard he was at Cedar Sinai in West Hollywood with throat cancer. I could only think of what he and Altovice must be going through. It was too painful to think of. Sammy had been great to me. He was a good friend. Even if I didn't speak or see him for months at a time, I always knew he was somewhere in the world working. How could this have happened to him? I called the hospital to see if there was anything I could do. I would have donated whatever body part he needed to help heal him. They said there was nothing to be done. He had asked to go home. I remembered once at a sit-down, the guys were laughing and saying to me, "You're going to outlast all of us. So we're going to make you the keeper of the key. You'll have to take care of us when we're all gone. You know, bring flowers and keep the headstones clean, stuff like that." They laughed. Sammy said, "Come on, kid, it's a joke."

It was the middle of May in 1990, and Sammy had gone. I couldn't believe the man with all that life was gone. He had enough life for ten people. I missed him already. I loved him. A few weeks later, a key arrived to a place at Forrest Lawn in Glendale. Years later our home in Mount Washington would overlook Forest Lawn. I brought flowers and polished the headstones of Sammy, Sam Sr., and Will Mastin. Sammy said the clothes they wore in their shows were spotless. So their headstones would be too, I'd see to that.

More and more I missed the business, and everyone I had known and loved growing up were gone. It seemed so strange to me, to have been talking to these people who were no longer here. Friends and people I had admired from afar and gotten the opportunity to be with them, up close and personal. Domino had started to dance with a promotion recording company and their new artist. I thought that was good for her. I knew she missed using her talents, and I didn't mind being with the children when she was away. This was good, maybe it would help mend some of the problems we were having financially. At least one of us was back at what we loved.

I had not opened my mouth to sing in years. I didn't doubt that I still could, there was just no reason to, and it had been so long. The nightmares were still there, and I suspected they would never go away.

Two years later, we were having another baby. It's not that we had money now, so this was the worst time to have a baby. Domino wanted a boy, and the doctor said this would probably be her last opportunity, and her last child by caesarean section. She gave birth to Gianni, an eight-pound boy.

Things were stretched. We had no money, and I had no job prospects. David, a writer friend of mine, rented us a house that he was in the process of selling. Domino's mother, meanwhile, had told her that she needed God in her life, that she needed to focus on positive things. There didn't seem to be any positive things in our marriage. She wanted out, and I didn't know what I wanted. I spent most of our marriage trying to forget the decisions we'd made and face the fact that she now feared me and forget that she had loved that guy. All of this was in my mind. I wanted to keep the family together, but at what cost to her?

I was no saint in our marriage. I knew my sin was the lack of love, the lack of showing emotions and feelings. She needed to be held and touched, and I didn't know how to give her that. I don't think she understood that I didn't desire to be with anyone else. She figured if I didn't want her, maybe I wanted someone else.

"Maybe you're confused," she would say, "Men or women, blonde hair, blue eyes, some skinny white girl."

I wasn't confused. I hated my life, my existence. I couldn't support my family. Maybe they would be better off without me. Why had I not let her go when she was in love with someone else? She could have had a chance to be happy. I thought about years earlier when I had walked into the ocean. There were those thoughts again. I figured I had to get enough life insurance to cover the family so when I was gone, they could make it. I didn't understand this life that I had. I didn't know what I was doing. The show had always been my place to go, a place that was safe. God, I just wanted to be safe again. I knew in my heart that the audience or my need to be with them was not real, but it was real to me. I moved their hearts with songs, emotions that I could only use in front of them.

Meanwhile, Domino was looking for a way to leave with her every move. She would pray, *why did God put me in this loveless marriage with this man? I just want to kill him and get it over with.* She would find yet another relationship to help her with her need to be loved. I could understand the need; I needed the audience and their love. We were both looking for love to help with the emptiness. She was planning her way out of the marriage, and I was just lost.

I should have never listened to Betty. Why did I marry and take on these responsibilities? The very things that I wasn't good at.

I couldn't understand these feelings that I had. Were they due to a lack of love growing up? I don't know. These were the things you heard on TV or at some doctor's office laying on a sofa. It wasn't real to the average person. It wasn't Domino or the children or our situation, but it was all-consuming. I wasn't on stage, and I wasn't happy, I couldn't find myself.

I kept on thinking it was all the jobs and taking the advice to leave show business, something I had known, something I believed in. I never believed I was good at sales, even though we had made out okay sometimes. The job was gone, and it was hard for me to find something else. I was determined to find something that would keep the family together and that would not have me all over the country, especially not at a time when Domino and I weren't on the same page about anything. I never blamed her for the love she needed; I knew she needed to be loved, and I couldn't give it to her.

One day Domino met a man on the bus, Gary Booker. Gary was a tall, thin black man in his early twenties. He worked for a stock brokerage firm in downtown Los Angeles. She'd been reading the Bible when he approached her and asked what she was reading. She'd decided to read the Bible from start to finish. He invited her to church.

She began attending services and always took the children with her. I never attended. I couldn't understand God, so I thought I would stay away from prayers and religion. I didn't need that to add to my problems. Domino started studying the Bible with a mind to be baptized and change her life. She had found peace, and it was good. She knew I would never come to a Christian church because I had lived and believed in the Jewish faith. It was all I knew, even though my family hadn't been Jewish. She always knew the difference in our faiths would be even more of a reason to separate, and she'd found her way out. Peace had come over her, just not the peace she had expected. She hadn't forgiven, and she hadn't exactly been truthful in her openness about her affairs and that her heart was consumed with divorce. If she were to be a true Christian, she would have to confront those things.

She moved forward. She was at peace, and I began to see her peace. I thought, how could she be at peace when I was in turmoil with life? We moved from a house to an apartment. The people from the church helped with the move, and they would come to the apartment to continue her studies. It had been about five months, and we were invited to dinner with a couple, John and Cecilia Coin, from the church. They wanted to take a better look at me and see if they could interest me in studying the Bible.

We had dinner and began to talk about what people believed, and they asked me how I came to be considered more Jewish than anything else. We looked at the Bible, and John kept saying, "Wait until we get to the part when you see what Jesus did for us."

My mother had been Baptist, and my father was Catholic. The rest of us were nothing. After spending as much time as I had with the Feldman's, I preferred Judaism.

Domino's peace was still being challenged by our lack of marriage. She was seeing great marriages in the church, and she didn't have one. She had a husband, but she was alone at church and at home. I was alone in my heart and soul. I was on a destiny with death. I wanted to end the agony of life. I thought my father must have been right when he said, "You will never be nothing," and I was nothing. Maybe he laid a curse on me with his words. I had a wife and children, and I was nothing. I couldn't support them, and as far as Domino was concerned, I didn't love them, or I would have left them. I had worked five or six jobs that didn't pay enough to cover anything

It was about midnight. My sleeping habits hadn't changed. I was still a night person. A doctor had once said, "Your internal clock is off schedule, but it will change back." It never did. It seemed to me, my time in music had passed; everything on the radio was just sounds. What had ever happened to being well rounded in the business, being able to do a little bit of everything?

I was through with life at this point. I had no four-hundred-dollar boots to leave on the beach this time. I was going to drive off the road in Malibu. As I was going west up Sunset Blvd. and passing all the spots I had performed at ten years earlier, my eyes were full of tears, and my heart and mind were consumed with death. As I drove through Beverly Hills, I thought about Sammy being at his home and how we had laughed. He was gone; the world I had known was gone. I was depressed and devastated. I thought about Domino and the children and the dinner with John and Cecilia. The words he kept saying, "Wait until we get to the part where you see what Jesus did for us," stayed in my head all the way to the coast. I turned onto Pacific Coast Highway and started to go north, passing "Gladstone's by the Sea," Domino's favorite restaurant. Everything I passed was a memory. I looked at the ocean and at what was to come that night.

In my mind, I kept hearing John saying over and over, "What Jesus did for us." I just wanted to die. I was so unhappy, so lost in the lack of what was real. I cried all night, thinking of the past, friends, and life. I sat at the beach parked in my car all night. It was four-thirty when I called John. I took a shuddering breath and tried to hold back the tears because it was hard to speak with the thoughts that consumed me. After a few minutes of trying to stop crying, John said, "Just take your time."

It was so softly spoken, it brought about a calm over me, and I said, "Okay, John, what did Jesus do for us?" I told him where I was and what I was doing. He asked me to hold on and not to do anything until he had a chance to speak with me in person. He said my problems were too big for him, but not too big for God and not too big for the other guy he wanted me to meet. He asked if I needed him to come to me or could I drive home?

He called me four times that day. "I wanted to see if you were okay, I hope you don't mind that I'm checking on you." He'd talked to Willie Flores, an Evangelist from the church, and had set up an appointment for the three of us to meet. We met at Willie's home in Pasadena at eight o'clock that evening. Willie Flores was a man in his forties and had been a major drug user in his youth. He had come close on many occasions to taking his own life and ruining his marriage. He had been a Christian for fifteen-plus years and had seen God do amazing things in people's lives.

He asked me if I was there to save my marriage or my life. I answered my life. My marriage was already gone. He said, "Good, sit down. I can help. If you were here to save your marriage, I couldn't help, but your life I can help you save."

We spent the next four hours reading the Bible and talking about my life. He said, "Don't leave anything out. I want you to talk openly about everything. I want you to write down your personal sins, not the sins of others that was done to you, but the sins that you committed. It's your life that you need to save." He continued, "You will need to learn to forgive and to ask for forgiveness, and I need you to commit to all of the sessions we're going to go through so you can understand God's grace and his sacrifice for you."

It was an emotional evening. I hadn't talked of these things in my life to anyone, and it took a lot out of me to express it. The next three sessions would show my lack of knowledge of the Christian Bible and of God. It was great to learn the message of the Bible and to understand God's plans for my life, how I had ruined those plans by the choices I'd made. I was starting to come out of my depression, there seemed to be light at the end of the tunnel.

My marriage and life at home with Domino hadn't changed much. Domino still wanted a divorce. She was glad that I had found God's promises, but that didn't change her having no feelings for me. The women she had studied with were telling her that she could have a great marriage now that we were on the same page, the same walk with God. Domino had lived this life, and they couldn't understand what she had been through: the disappointments, the mental and emotional abuse, and the lack of love she had lived with for over seven years. They didn't know she had wanted me dead, and now she just wanted out.

I wanted now to save what we had left and rebuild for the future. We had a chance to save our marriage, but she wasn't willing. The ladies were running out of scriptures to call her to see the light, so they called Willie to counsel her. After meeting with him, it made a difference in what she would say, but not what she would feel and what she would do.

A few weeks later, I was baptized. It was an incredible feeling that I was starting over with people who were now family and the relationships we now had. I had been so alone and isolated in my life, but the walls that had been built so high were now coming down, and it felt right. Finally it seemed I could put the demons behind me. It had been a year of studying the Bible and meeting with others studying. Sometimes I led the study, just as Willie had done with me.

One night around three am after a study, I must have been in a deep sleep when suddenly I woke up. I realized the nightmare had stopped. One day it was just no longer there.

Domino and I were partnered with four other couples that discussed their marriages openly. We all helped each other with day-to-day life as husband and wife per the way the Bible said marriage should be. Our children were with other children in the ministry, and they were doing great. We moved into a new home that would suit our family, and it was still close enough to the other couples so we could be near each other for support.

A couple of years had gone by, and we were to attend a marriage retreat. Then the classes would continue for six weeks, ending in a dinner celebration with entertainment. Ron and Cindy Marsh, who led the marriage retreat, were also in charge of the ministry that oversaw the music for the church. The church had eight thousand members, broken up into sectors throughout Southern California. They wanted to do something a little different, so they were calling around to the different ministries to see what they could put together or whom they could get, when Domino threw my name into the hat.

"Donn is a great singer," she told Ron. "He's sung on stage in nightclubs, Las Vegas, and the Hollywood Bowl."

Ron said, "Why isn't he singing at church?"

"He doesn't do it anymore or won't do it anymore. He doesn't think God wants him to sing."

Ron said, "I'll call him later and ask if he'd do it. Maybe we can talk him into it."

The night of the dinner was a weekend away, and Ron called me about singing. It had been seven years since I had opened my mouth to sing, other than singing Sammy or Frank's songs around the house for the kids. I agreed to do this, and I had nothing to sing. Ron asked me if I could do something a little different, not gospel or even a Christian song, but something that would be romantic, just right for the evening.

The night of the event, I had pulled out some of Tony Bennett's material. When you say love songs, Tony B's are still the songs to fall in love to. I had arranged to sing with prerecorded tracks to save time. I hadn't worked with a pianist, and there was no time to. The event was to take place at a home in Pasadena, a garden setting. It was intimate, but they were still far enough away from me to meet my comfort zone. They were an audience.

I began to sing the first song and got through the verse. They started applauding. They were looking at Domino and saying, is he lip syncing? Domino had always heard me singing a little around the house, but this was different. Later she would say, "It was so beautiful, so polished, so in control."

I finished the first song, and the applause was warm. People were saying, "I thought he was lip synching. He really sounds like that, that wasn't a recording?"

I finished the next two songs. The night air was warm, and the feeling was unbelievable. Something had breathed life into me, which I had not felt in years.

Ron said, "You have got to sing at church. We're going to be at the Wiltern Theater, and you must plan a song for the communion service.

My sister Betty had always said, "For a black man, you don't have soul in your singing." So, I stayed away from church singing.

Ron said, "I can't wait to tell the Region Leader about how you sing."

It was right to feel so at home. I was comfortable in front of an audience. I had lived there all my life. But I wasn't yet ready to commit to singing. What was I doing? I didn't want God to think he had saved my life so I could sing and stand before others in the church in a position of righteousness. But as time went on, I was asked to sing more and more. The Shrine, the Wiltern, and places I had sung at years earlier. It felt so strange, and yet, so right to stand on those stages.

The more I sang, the more it came back to me, and the ability to move hearts was more apparent. People would come up to me with tears and hug me and say, "When you sing those songs, it's as though you're telling a story. It's like we are there."

I felt as though I was a better performer than I'd been years earlier. Barriers had been broken. Things had changed for the better.

Domino and I still had major problems with intimacy. I still couldn't be what she needed. She wanted and needed emotional love, and I had lost emotion so many years ago. I seemed only to have emotion and feeling in front of an audience with a song, not at home with her. She knew of my history, at least some of it, but it didn't make up for what she needed in our marriage and our relationship.

We were now leading a "bible talk" of marrieds and some singles that were dating. It was a combination of our old group when we first came into the church and other couples we had studied the bible with who had become Christians. We had what was the fun group, Mr. and Mrs. Hollywood, as we were referred to. Now, I didn't know the details of two more affairs that she'd had, but I suspected. I thought that our problems were more in regular husband and wife kind of problems, but that shows how out of touch most husbands are about their wives or to women in general and their needs. You know how you just know something, but you have no visible proof? Well, that's how I felt. Our lives had moved on and yet, we were still in the same position. She needed to be loved so much, and I was behind the walls that had been my life support. I couldn't tell her what had happened to me. I had buried it so deep that it had been there chasing me through my life.

Chapter 11: Something from Nothing

Domino was again pregnant, and we were at odds because we couldn't afford another child nor could we sustain a marriage the way she was feeling about our relationship. We limped along and in a few months, we had our fourth child, Sasha. She was born three months too soon, one pound, nine ounces, and she was perfect. The child neither of us was sure we wanted.

Sasha was tiny, but everything worked. The cord had been wrapped around her neck, and she was breach, so they went in and took her. She spent the next three months in the hospital. That was strange, going through a pregnancy and then going to the hospital and coming home empty-handed. Domino and I were on different schedules, so we visited at different times. She would go during her lunch hour, and I would go late evenings around eleven pm.

It was great to be there. It would be feeding time, and all the babies would be crying. I'd sing Sinatra songs, and they would all calm down. The nurses couldn't believe it. They looked forward to me singing and to the visits. They'd say, "Are you singing anywhere where we could see you?"

"Yeah, here every night about eleven pm, the second show."

Then I would leave my little Sasha. I would drive around thinking of my life and how it was so different. The life I missed, the audiences, Las Vegas, and my crazy life with Curtis. I missed him so much. He was now touring around the world, singing with the Platters, a group from the sixties and seventies. Nostalgia shows, but he was working. I thought about Domino, I thought we were okay-not great, but okay.

We brought Sasha home. Four great children, and our home was quiet. We enjoyed being together, laughing, playing games, and having family devotional. It never occurred to me at the time how different our home was from the one I grew up in. As a father, I was a very different man than my own. If I'd thought of this, I might have felt more encouraged. Our home was beautiful and for the first time, we were not being evicted.

Gabrielle had asthma and skin problems from the time she was born. The doctor said she was at fifty percent of her breathing capacity and that we needed to leave the state or at least move to a beach community. We didn't give it a second thought. We found a beach community in Ventura County and within a month, we moved. The company I worked for went through a merger, and I lost my job again. The timing was terrible.

Gabrielle was about ten or eleven and doing great; she was on the basketball team, and her grades went from practically failing to getting B's. It was a good move. She was safe, she was breathing, and her skin was clearing up. This would be the first time I would consider going back on stage. How and where would I begin? I didn't know. All the contacts that I had were long gone. I had no music, no show to sell; Lambert had gone to New York years ago. I had no booking agents, no manager, and no arrangements.

Week after week went by with no job and no way of getting back to the music and the audience I loved so much. The Latin sector at church was planning a women's day event and thought it would be nice if they did a big dance segment and utilized couples to do a Tango. Domino was called out to choreograph the number, but she wasn't familiar with the tango, so she suggested they ask me. "Donn use to teach ballroom dances," she said. I agreed, and Domino and I met with the couples. I spent about a month teaching them the steps, and then I choreographed the dance. The night was beautiful. The Latin ministry certainly knew how to have fun, and the dance was a huge success. I could still create dance and choreograph. My singing voice was better than ever, but it still was not my time.

I got a call from the father of a young man who had been in our old Bible talk group in Los Angeles. His son Aubrey had a brain aneurysm and was on life support. Aubrey and I had spoken every week since we left Los Angeles,

144

but this week I hadn't heard from him. He was in a hospital in Pasadena and wasn't going to make it. At his bedside were his wife Nadine, their mothers, and his father, and a host of friends from church. I looked at him in bed with no motion at all. The doctor said he was already gone. It was just a question now of life support and the decision that his wife and family needed to make. They'd been married eleven months and were planning their first anniversary. I prayed and prayed as I stood in the outer hallway hoping for what I had heard to be miracles, but there were to be no miracles this night. He was gone.

Everything that was in me died that night. I was lost in my self-pity and in the loss of this young man. What was God doing with all the hurt and suffering that went on in the world? What was the sense of taking this young man? I couldn't understand the suffering people had to endure before God would step in. I looked at the Bible and read through some stories of others suffering and threw the Bible away. There couldn't be a God that would allow this. These were just stories that didn't help. This young man was dead, and his young wife was left with no children to comfort her. It seemed there was nothing to show for her eleven-month marriage. What did God leave her with? My thoughts were consumed with anger towards this God who would allow suffering beyond reason.

As the days went by, I called Nadine to ask her what she might need, and I told her that if she wanted, I would sing at the funeral. She said she wanted me to, but she knew how much I loved Aubrey and thought it might be too hard for me. I told her it was hard, but I would do it. I had just sung at their wedding eleven months ago, and now I would sing a song I hadn't done since junior high school graduation, "He Ain't Heavy, He's My Brother."

The funeral was large. In his eight years in the church, Aubrey had known hundreds of people, and they were there to say good-bye and show their respect to his wife and family.

As for me, my depression grew worse, and with no income, we were in the process of another eviction. It was happening again. Everything was taking its toll on our marriage, and it was coming to an end. How long could we stumble along together while she wanted out? She was through with the lack of love for all those years, and I was now ready to agree.

A position opened at General Telephone Directories in their sales department of advertising, and I took the job. We struggled along, but it was over. Domino, in her thoughts, was a single mom and one day might marry a Christian man without the background and the baggage that I had. A year went by, as we struggled through our relationship. I had given up on everything that was of a spiritual nature and resolved to live and take each day as it came, no expectations of anything. Any day my marriage might end for good, or we might be living on the streets, or I might lose another job, or I might get a brain aneurism and fall down dead. I just didn't care.

At this point, I didn't care about how God felt about me or anyone else. For instance, I thought I was being discreet, but I forgot how intuitive Domino could be. She taped a phone conversation between me and a friend speaking of escapades in the past. She thought it was currently going on. Later she told me that my behavior toward her was so erratic that it was easy to believe it was happening now. When she first confronted me, I denied everything. She'd known I would, that's why she taped the phone conversation. It was clear to me that if things had come to that, I should grant her the divorce. She'd earned it.

I wanted to tell the children of our plans. I got them out of bed and sat them down at the breakfast table. As I began to tell them about the plans, the look on their face was of total confusion. They ate their breakfast and prepared for school. What was usually a fun kind of question-and-answer ride to school about anything and everything was, that day, very quiet.

I knew that this time she was determined, and I was fine in accepting it. In the days ahead, the heaviness of our marriage was lifted. For some reason, the pain of all those years was gone, and we started getting along better. We could laugh and talk about things that were taboo and that we had left unsaid in earlier times. It seemed our relationship changed when we stopped trying so hard or when we stopped thinking of it as something we needed to fix. We were friends helping each other through things. I had let go of her, and I was okay. I would still be a father, that would never change, and I would be alone and that could have its advantages. I had started to think about music, and I was at my best when I was alone and working on music. It was unreal to think that this talk of divorce was making us feel great about ourselves. I was coming to terms with the idea.

We began looking for separate homes that would accommodate her and the children. I only needed one room. A month or so had gone by, and we were laughing and having a good time at home for the first time in a long time.

The children didn't understand that the reason things were so light was because the heaviness had gone. We were separate in our thoughts for each other, so there was no pressure. This went on for a time and then one evening her mother called.

Her mother, with whom I had bridged the gap with years back, told her, "He will be a lost soul on this earth if you leave him. You are his tie to life and to God."

Her statement to Domino made her have compassion for me. She looked at all that I had lived through, and she looked deep in herself and said, "God, you have kept me with this man all these years. I have been running for years; I need to love him and help him to love me the way I need to be loved. He is the father of our children and the man you gave me to live with and love the rest of my life."

We sat down and recommitted our life to each other with a willingness to be open about our feelings, whatever they might be. At this point, Domino started to really look at her life and that maybe true love had eluded her because she was not being real to God nor to the women in her bible group he had put in her life. She thought it was time to be open about the affairs she'd had and the things that she had never confessed in hopes to be right with God. She was scared that it would change things with us now that we had decided to have a fresh start. All that time she didn't understand it had nothing to do with me not loving her, but that the love I had for her I couldn't get to because of all the pain and the things that had happened to me as a child and a young man. I couldn't come from behind the wall. She told of the affairs, not knowing how I was going to react. I would either leave her or forgive her and stay. She didn't try to excuse her behavior or justify her actions. I never held it against her. It was my doing or my lack of doing that took a beautiful young woman and made her doubt her very being. She was beautiful and married to someone who didn't make her feel beautiful or loved. Somehow we had endured all those years, and we were together. Two months later, we bought a home and moved the family in. Life had made a change, and I even started to return to church with the family.

Frank Sinatra's death would now send me in a tailspin. I had seen him in one of his last concerts at the Long Beach Arena. He was still everything he'd always been. The ballads were so smooth, and he was Frank at his best, funny and dynamic, and a real force on stage. He had a few years earlier signed a photograph for me, "To Donn, All the Best, Frank Sinatra." All I had left of these fabulous people were photos- Judy Garland, Totie Fields, Ella Fitzgerald, Pearl Bailey, Sammy, and now Frank. These people were great in their talent and just regular nice people, always willing to give a leg up to someone, secure in their talent and good people to be around. I had met Totie through the Feldman's and Ella and Pearl when I was about twelve years old at a party in Hollywood. When I first got to Las Vegas, Totie was like a Jewish mother. At eighteen, I would audition for Pearl Bailey's, "Hello Dolly" at the Music Center and was an honorary escort for Ella at an NAACP event. All three of these warm and beautiful women had one thing in common. When they saw me, they all tried to feed me. Judy had been gone since 1969. Sammy went too young, and Frank was Father Time. It wasn't easy to look back and see them all gone.

A year earlier, I had met a woman at church. Her son was a member who'd heard me sing and who'd heard about my singing on stage in Las Vegas. He wanted his mother to play for me at service and told me that she was a very good musician. A few weeks later, I was working on a new song for church and remembered the conversation. I called his home and met with his mother, Roberta Lydecker.

He was right, not only being a good musician, but she was a great arranger and a conductor. Roberta was no stranger to the business; one of the Lydeckers had won an Academy Award in cinematography, and she had made the rounds on tour in Europe and in concert. I would meet with her at her home in Ventura, a modest home with no pretense. She was just a classy lady with a huge talent. She and I would talk for hours about the business and the changes we'd seen over the years. If we were going to do something, the timing was right. She asked me about the music I used to do, and I said "I don't really do the music I used to do. I have an idea that I've been kicking around, and I've been looking for an arranger who can pull it off."

She said, "I'd like to try."

I gave her the music and my concept, and she began to work creatively. Over the next twelve months, we would work on music of all styles. She would begin to craft the arrangements with thick harmonies and rich cords, but we had no direction with the music. Months went by, and she called me over to hear what she had done. It wasn't what I was looking for. It was still like what I had heard in the past. She went back to work. A month later, she called me back to her home to listen to a song I had given her. It was a Frank Sinatra song from the forties, "This Love of Mine." It had a new arrangement, and I wrote a new melody with harmonies around the old melody. It was beautiful; she had written and arranged what I had been looking for, what I dreamt of hearing for years.

I was excited about the prospect of the new sound keeping the integrity of the original way the music was done, but bringing it into the twenty-first century. It seemed a tall order for someone who was not equipped, but Roberta was. She was brilliant, and she could master the arrangements to suit my vocal ability. I said to her, "Roberta, right now you are a one-song wonder. You have to be able to do it again."

She did. She finished the second song, and we decided to record the two songs as a calling card. We now had a package, and she had started to work on the other music. Eleven Sinatra songs and a one and a two-hour concert, which would include rock, latin jazz, rhythm and blues, and musical comedy. No one black at least was doing it. It seemed they had made room for us. I was about to have an opportunity to use all I had learned, not to be a star that was fleeting, but to be a working entertainer again and to love and support my family (which now included Roberta and her family).

We were a team and soon to be a force in the business. I was that sure of her arrangements; it was the right time for us. I had come full circle. Roberta and I had similar lives, things like violence and lack of support when we needed it the most. We had both walked away from the thing we loved the most, and it was that thing that gave us breath. It was a gift, and it was what God had wanted us to do, use the talent. Domino was set to co-choreograph, and we would take our family on the road.

It had been four years, and I was still with General Telephone. They were talking of a merger. This was a scary thing. Company mergers had meant unemployment for me twice before. The fallout to home and family had always been tough. Could our fragile, newly-reborn marriage survive it again? This time was different. We owned our home (well, at least the bank owned it), no landlords. The merger took place, and it happened again. I was out of a job. Thank God, we still had our dreams.

The music was finished, and so was the show. There was fine-tuning that needed to be done; a few weeks of rehearsal would take care of that. Things had started to get tight. We needed to sell our home so we could complete the recording of the music. I lost almost one hundred thousand dollars with that merger, so our finances were almost down to nothing. We scrambled to sell the house as soon as possible, but the bottom was falling out of the market.

Our marriage was at ninety percent, the music was great, and the promise of working and our children traveling with us kept us happy. As the months went by, the notices started to come with the certainty of foreclosure. It was getting scarier all the time. We began to think, *what are we going to do?* If we could finish the music and the show and sell it, we would be fine. We decided we needed to find a way of getting back in the business in a big way. We needed a TV show that would put us on the map and get the ball rolling. The old variety shows were all gone, but there were still talk shows. We needed to get the package finished.

The country went through an attack on our soil, the World Trade Center in New York was demolished, and thousands were killed. What now? So much hurt, so much hurt. People turned to God for faith and for hope, and I turned to the music. I loved simpler times when music simply said, "I love you." People need to know they're loved and that there's hope and that faith is the beginning of that hope.

There were slim food days around the house for six people. Domino and I kept finding temporary jobs, but the job market was slim, and people were losing their jobs left and right. Somehow we were making it. Domino was teaching hip-hop at different schools, and that helped quite a bit. As I write this, we are thirteen days from foreclosure and no buyers for our home.

I sat down to write down my thoughts one night about eleven-thirty when I couldn't sleep and wrote my whole life. I had forgotten so many things about my life, and so many of the things poured into my thoughts. I had thought that most of it was a bad nightmare for so many years. As I started to write, it started coming back to me, and I couldn't stop the history that was unfolding before me. It was my life.

I had forgotten my mother saying, "Show no emotion, no fear." The wall that protected me was the very wall that kept all others out, even Domino and the children (and probably Liz many years earlier). I remembered those men, and I hadn't thought of them in years. I could remember their conversation, the very words they said to me, about me, in that room. I always just returned to school as though nothing had happened. For me the only thing wrong was the smell and the filth. We didn't see PG-13 or R-rated movies in the sixties. There were no commercials on child abuse or molestation. Those subjects weren't talked about. I was taught to do these things with these men as though it was natural for every kid. I sat down to write my thoughts that evening after hearing a message from a man who had studied the Bible with me some ten years earlier, and I wrote thirty-five pages by hand throughout the night.

It was eight o'clock in the morning, and my children were coming down to breakfast. I was in tears and a mess. My daughter Gabrielle asked, "Are you okay, Dad?"

The pages were all over the floor. Domino came in. "Have you been down here all night?" She picked up the pages. "What is this?"

I told her that I couldn't sleep and came down to write my thoughts, and this was the result. I wrote about events in my life. She asked to read them. She said, "You've never been able to write more than one line." I wasn't ready for her to read it yet, but when it was complete, I would, maybe, if I could complete it.

I started writing in those thirty-five pages about my father's funeral and then how I felt about his death. Then I remembered no emotion, no fear and no feelings, and how I came to be this way. As I wrote about how I felt, I began to shake uncontrollably. I had a sense of a smell that was foul. I remembered those men in that room and what they were doing to me. I was amazed at what I was remembering all a sudden-what they said and what they smelled like and the look and smell of the room. It was all in my head thirty-five years later. I never had thought of this stuff, I never wanted to. Now it was as though it was yesterday in my mind. I lost a sense of time and perspective. Suddenly, it was dark in the room. I could hear their voices. I could feel them touching me, pulling me to them. It was as though someone turned on the movie, and it was all being shown to me in full color. There were no missing spaces in what I was remembering. I remembered everything that was said and done.

I realized that the nightmares I had and the anxiety which led to shortness of breath and chest pains were due to those memories in my head. All the time I was running from those shadows chasing me and waking up in a cold sweat was due to these visions in my head. I was so cold and unfeeling about everything. I never put it together that this stuff was the cause. Whenever it happened, I simply returned to the stage. I never stopped to think about what it might be doing to me.

I was now at sixty handwritten pages and decided it was time to move to a word processor. Hand-writing this was hard. After about a week of different things coming to mind, I decided to start at the beginning. The more I wrote, the more the memories came to mind and the more pain I would remember. I was like a madman at the computer putting down my thoughts.

So now I was writing this on one hand and working on a show on the other, totally consumed, still not fully understanding the reality of what happened to me. I couldn't get a job, and the only thing that was working was the completion of the show and the music and the frantic thoughts that were now coming to mind. There had seemed to always be something going on in my life to deflect what was going on. As a young performer, there was the stage, and now there were the problems of life and family. It put all that had happened to me once again on the back burner. Maybe it had been so many years ago, it didn't make a difference, I don't know.

The days clicked on, and time had run out on our home. We had dropped the price ninety-thousand dollars and still had no offers. Now if we sold it, it would barely pay broker fees and some fifteen thousand dollars' worth of personal debts. We didn't owe a great deal, but we still needed enough from the sale to rent a house until things improved. It would come down to a sale to a real-estate investor who would take the property at bottom price and give us a credit to move into one of his rental properties. I had to find a way to move the family into a home, and I had no income. It was the holiday season, and we were just grateful that we'd found the investor.

"God, I need to support the family," I prayed.

It was hard signing our home over to a man who made silly jokes about other people's lives. This meant the debts we had would remain outstanding

152

because the sale of the home to him would only pay off the bank. He said, "Well, at least you won't have a foreclosure on your credit report, but you're not going to make any money."

A week later, the bank added additional fees that would cancel the deal. Our home would sell at a trustee sale if I couldn't find another buyer and fast. I had nowhere to turn, and no money to move the family. I was working a part-time job that barely kept food on the table and the utilities paid. The words I had heard as a child rang in my head, "YOU'LL NEVER BE NOTHING!" Was it true? I could hardly think positive about this. It was another loss. It was ten days before Christmas, a time that we would normally be shopping for gifts for homeless children. This time it would be my children. It was scary. What would I say to our children?

They had Christmas lists that included three gifts. They wanted nothing major, CD's and little things and a gift from each of them to the children at the Christmas toy drive. I longed for the days when I could retreat to the stage, the lights, and the people wanting to love me for what I was good at: entertaining. That was my inner me trying to get back to where it was safe. God had given me a talent, and I needed to find a way to use it.

Ten days before Christmas, we returned from church. It was evening, and we put the children to bed. We looked through the homes for rent section of the newspaper trying to find a place to live. We had no money, and we were going to be out of food for the children's lunches that Monday morning. There wasn't a lot of hope, but we looked anyway.

The next morning, Domino went to take the children to school and dashed out to start the car, and the car was gone. We had sent one payment, but we were three behind, and the car was repossessed. This year had taken its toll; we had no way financially to combat all we were going through.

The children had now noticed that they had no Christmas tree and began to look worried. Gabrielle asked, "Don't we normally have our tree up by now?"

I had no answer, what could I say to her? We still had a few days left. Domino and I kept searching the papers for jobs, but with the economy and the job market, we could only hope that things would turn around before we were in the street. I think the children would have noticed that. It would be hard to convince them we were camping out under a highway overpass just to have a family adventure. It had been years since I had no worries about finances. There was always another show, and I'd had only myself to take care of. Now I experienced fear at its worst.

The children were starting to catch winter colds. We had no insurance for doctors. We could only pray, and I was almost all prayed out. I tried to hold onto the faith that so many had talked about, but it was disappearing day by day as the losses kept coming in-the job, the house, and the car. I felt pain in my chest and had not slept for days.

It had been so long; most of my relationships in the business had long gone or passed away. The music wasn't finished. I needed a little more financing to complete the manufacturing of the CD's, and they wouldn't be finished for another two weeks. Maybe I had enough done. If I had the right person to hear what I was doing, maybe I could get some backing. At least enough to try to move into a rental until February when I had a few club dates promised. Everyone who had heard the two songs raved about how beautiful they were and how the sound was right for now.

I had so much on my plate. I couldn't think which direction to go first. I needed to find a way to take care of our housing before the bank put us out on the street. I didn't know where to begin or who to begin with. I called a man I hadn't seen in over ten years to show him what I was working on.

David was a tall, thin man, gray hair, soft-spoken with a gentle smile. He had helped me in the past, but it had been years. I went to his home in the Hollywood Hills, a large house, gated, with lush grounds. His home was that of an English Estate-art and statues. The sitting room had a grand piano and hardwood floors and center carpets and books and paper, it had the smell of paper. David was a producer and a writer of plays and music. He listened to what was going on in my life since we had last spoken. We spoke of my children and the fact that there were now four.

I played the music for him. He, like everyone else who'd heard it, liked it and said he thought it would please that forty-plus audience and that it had a shot at making it.

David said, "Let me give your situation some thought, and I'll get back to you in a few days."

We shook hands, said our good-byes, and he walked me to the door. I almost didn't ask him for help, but I had come this far. He was a man of means, but he was a man who, like a select few in the world, was very down-to-earth with no pretense or greatness, just a regular guy. I went home to wait.

Once again we had found someone to buy the house, another investor. This would be even less money, but at least it would pay off the house and pay off a couple of personal debts. We spent Christmas Day driving around the neighborhood in Woodland Hills looking at "for rent" signs. This area was expensive. The rent in the Los Angeles area had almost doubled since we last lived there.

Domino had been asking me about the writing. I wasn't ready to share it yet. I was still learning all the things I had put away, put out of mind. I had begun to spend so much time at the computer writing that she and the children were all asking about "the book" as they called it. Was it a book? Until then I hadn't thought of it as anything but my own tangled thoughts given release on paper. I gave her the first draft of the pages in hand writing. She took the pages and went away.

That evening she came to me and said, "I thought I was going to skim through it, but I couldn't put it down. It just kept on peaking my interest. Not just because it was your life, but it read so sensitively that it kept pulling me along."

My hopes and my dreams were all riding on the possibility of a great life and on the possibility of going back to work in a business that I loved. But we weren't there yet. It was seven days before Christmas, and Domino took the children to a midweek Christmas party at church. A friend had loaned us his car to get them there. We were trying, but it was getting tougher every day to hold it together. My children understood what Christmas meant. They knew it was about people and caring, not toys and waste. They knew that there were people, especially children, who were always left out. They always wanted to make sure they thought of other children now and always remembered to pray for them. I knew for that reason alone, listening to Sasha, the five-year-old praying that Jesus help the kids who didn't have a family or toys, I had to hold on. She prayed, and I cried. It was great to hear the truth about Christmas from a child who believed.

There was little food in the house, and I had an advertising sales job that wasn't producing much income, maybe because of the time of year, maybe because I was under the gun to make it work, maybe because I was never good at it. The pressure was so intense, I couldn't sleep. Every night for a week I was awake, walking the house. I knew one thing and believed it, God was in control. Thank you, God, because I had no control.

Roberta had composed great music, and if I could get the music heard, we'd be back at work and in a major way. The music was beautiful. However, we had to be out of the house by January 15th, 2002. We managed to find an apartment in Woodland hills, an area where the schools were good. Six people in a small, but okay, apartment. We were grateful.

It was time to move things forward, to turn up the heat. Things were moving too slow or maybe I was just impatient, but impatience was what I would use to turn this around. I knew there was no more waiting for something to happen. I had to make things happen. It was a new year, and I was determined to live. Last year had been a tough year, but there were great things that had happened. Now it was time to use some of those things. It would be our turn again. With all the struggling, there were tremendous blessing in our lives. Domino and I were in great shape, and we continued to work out with weights and through dance.

At forty-four, my weight was one hundred and fifty-five, down from one hundred and seventy-three pounds, and my waist was twenty-nine inches. Domino, at thirty-eight, had just won Miss Fitness, and she could still dance circles around dancers half her age. Her jazz and her hip-hop choreography gave dancers headaches trying to keep up with her. She had worked on a Jubilee 2000 Musical Production at the Great Western Forum and an equal, but smaller production in San Diego at the Concourse. My voice had gained momentum. It was mature, and my first tenor range had stood the test of time. All the things I had learned about being prepared for performance worked in the recording studio. It was spiritual. The music that I loved had come full circle.

It was time for beautiful music to once again take its place in the entertainment business, with voices that could sing in perfect harmony with that music. We began to put the packages together. I took new photos and dusted off the resume. The demo was complete. We had a new two-hour show that utilized twenty-two songs. There were five big production numbers. The style of music in the show consisted of latin jazz, rock, broadway, and rhythm and blues, lots of ballads. The show could be broken up into smaller twenty-minute or thirty-minute spots. Now to find the right venue.

I had always had personal management, someone else to take care of the basics. This time I would be doing it all myself. Las Vegas, Japan, or European engagements—was one the right direction or a combination of all? We began sending out demo packages to booking agents and record labels around the country. Email was a great tool because you could send out notices and information around the country and get responses within a day. I was more determined as the days went by to land something. I didn't know which direction was right, what venue to start first. I started with all of them. TV, radio, stage, nightclubs, concerts, opening act or headliner-one of these would be right.

I had endured the beatings from my father and the room with those men, a divorce, and a rape in a city I loved. So much had happened in the years past, a lifetime of rights and wrongs, successes and failures and disappointments. I had worked twenty-five jobs since leaving the stage. I had left what I loved and what had worked for me so many years earlier. God had walked me out of the water and kept me from the cliffs in Malibu. My father's words for so many years had haunted me, "You'll never be nothing."

"You'll never be nothing" was now in the distant past. Those words would never again have a place in my heart, my mind, or in my soul. I proved the words to be as worthless as the man who said them. I was something; I was going to be something. I always would be something. I was now more determined than ever to return to center stage. God help me get there.

Six months went by, and we had begun sending out the demo CD's. The response was great, but still slow. We previewed the CD to teens and thirty-five year olds, and they loved it. The teens were the big surprise. They were all falling in love with this music. They told us, "We were playing it all day long." They already knew all the words. It was great to hear this response from young people as they were not at all the target audience.

We had sent the music to all the major players. Some thirty managers and booking agents throughout the country. Merv Griffin Entertainment, Barbara Streisand at Barwood Productions, Phil Gersh of The Gersh Agency, Jay Leno and four Executive Producers at the Oprah Winfrey Show.

The first draft of a manuscript on my life was complete. It had become a crucial part of my return. I now knew and understood the whole story and had no fear as I relived it. It was a life that, given a choice, I would have chosen differently. But it was the life I lived.

June 3rd, 2002 at 5:30pm a call came from one of the executive producers at the "Oprah Winfrey Show." She was requesting an outline for me to appear on the show. This was the call Roberta and I had talked about two years earlier. I had no fear of telling the story. We knew Oprah; she had been in our home for years. There was a great feeling of trust in telling her the story. I felt she would protect me. Her show was all over the country. This was the shot that would do it. TV would give national appeal to the music. We proposed a day of love songs and a discussion of the manuscript I had written. We titled the theme, "A Man Who Dreamed." The dream was coming true and in a big way.

Things had changed a lot since the late seventies, going to Las Vegas, meeting Sammy, having his support and friendship. Getting a job in the clubs was different in those days. Seems like all you had to do was show up and there was work for a singer-dancer. Now you needed a video performance for them to review.

We were planning a PBS spot on a show called "Sound Affects." This would allow me to utilize the 28-piece orchestra, as well can talk about the concept of how the music and the sounds of the forties transformed. How the integrity of the piece was maintained. Getting this show would also give us more footage for the video and go a long way in visually giving us that look we wanted to portray on stage.

As we waited, Roberta decided to redo the strings section to make them more lush. After all, this was one of the main reasons the music was so different and had received such high praise from the listening audiences. It was simply beautiful. It had been almost six months of waiting, which is the nature of this business, "hurry up and wait." Everyone wants you to send it yesterday and then nothing. I needed to sing, somewhere!

I began to lose that faith that had once been so strong, holding on for such a long time. It was a battle that I could not understand. It appears God had given me the talent, but not the means to use it. What I needed to sustain me was any validation that what God had given me, he was allowing me to use. There was a time in this business when performers did what they did for the sheer love of it and the prospect that it would feed them. It had been a dream for such a long time.

I got a call to sing in a movie, a night club scene for an Independent film by Revelation Pictures called, "Seasons of Life," which Maramax Pictures was now interested in. The film's producer/director, Kristian Allen, heard the promo CD and thought the two songs we prepared for the demo were a perfect match for his film. They shot three singers in the club scene for the film, and all but my footage went to the cutting room floor in editing. That was good to hear, especially in film, since the cutting room floor was an occupational hazard.

I was getting calls for little things, luncheons for the Governor of California's wife Sharon Davis and an evening at the Beverly Wilshire and a few other club dates. The big prize was still waiting in the wings. We were sure that a TV appearance on the "Oprah Winfrey Show" would be a prayer answered. We'd now sent five copies of the manuscript to Oprah's producers. Ellen Ratiken, the supervising producer, said they couldn't accept the manuscript in its current form, but they were possibly interested in it for a segment. So from that time on, we would have an excerpt from the writing and a note about the music sent over to the producers. I needed to keep my name and my music on their desks and in their minds. The business had changed over the years, but not that much. You still had to pursue the target and continually push the issue. It wasn't going to be easy, but nothing worth having is. We now had quite a few things in the works. It would be an interesting year.

We turned our attention towards Las Vegas and a new show designed to showcase a live orchestra and sixteen dancers, all following my lead. This variety/night club show we were proposing to the Park Place Group. They controlled the Paris Hotel, The Flamingo Hilton, Caesars, and several other high profile casinos and entertainment theaters. We sent the same package to the Bellaggio/MGM-Mirage Group. A talent coordinator for the Jerry Lewis Telethon requested we submit a package for the 2003 show.

My sleeping habit of two to three hours a night was now part of how I functioned. I could stay awake up to five days and yes, be exhausted, but still not sleep. Sometimes you wonder how you can go on, but then you look into the eyes of an eleven-year-old who looks back at you and says, "I believe in you, Dad." I could hardly hold it all together. I knew I had to. I still believed in the dream and the gift. All we had to do was hold on, with Roberta conducting, and I would sing to an audience I missed and loved.

To my dearest Domino,

I write this letter to you in hope that you will forgive me. You have given me four beautiful children. You taught me to say I love you to our children, and I will always be grateful for that.

You are gentle and sweet and patient. Your love was so endearing, a love that was instilled in a little girl born in the Dominican Republic.

It was a treasure buried on an island that very few can have. Many find the treasure, but very few could possess it for their very own. You offered it to me, and I was one of those who could only admire it from afar. It was never to be mine to hold and cherish.

I ask your forgiveness for taking your breath, a life with love was the air you needed to breathe.

You endured separation in a relationship with me. I was supposed to honor you and protect you. As a man, that was supposed to be first and foremost in my heart. But as you know, it was not. Making love to you was to bring a passion to you that would bring glory to God. But as you know, it did not. You are beautiful and giving in all that you do and all that you are. As I said to you some eighteen year ago, "I don't want you to change, it's me who needs to change." I apologize for never changing

In looking back, I remembered a conversation with your mother. She was right. I realize the dark clouds she saw in my life were the very clouds that would destroy the love you deserved. She said, "I did not bring my daughter into this world to suffer." And suffer you did. I can, without any doubt, say, had I not been the man that I was, you would have never had to learn to endure without love.

My lack of ability to love you with passion and possession is the only reason you had to give up so much. I ask your forgiveness for not being a responsible and reliable husband and man to warrant the love of a woman who cared and gave as much as you.

Twenty years is a long time to put love on the back burner. I came in between what could have been a great love for you so many years ago. I realized when you feared me, although you tried, love was over.

I wish with all my heart that I could give you back what I took in destroying that relationship. What it must have felt like to have time stand still because the love you feel is present and so wonderful.

You'll Never Be Nothing

The beautiful Gabrielle,

You are my first daughter, and a daughter to whom I ask forgiveness. I have always wanted the best for you. I believe there are many failures in my attempt to provide security and protection for you. I have always wanted to secure a home and a financial freedom that would give you stability. I realize that you are smart and beautiful. I also realize that if I would have provided a more stable home for you, you would have been grounded in your studies. It is my responsibility to provide you with a comfort and a love that would help you to excel to heights that would secure a positive future in life. I always thought if you simply felt the love of your father, it might be enough until I could provide security for you. Having to move from area to area did not help with long term relationships for you, and again, I ask your forgiveness. I can only hope that you've known all these years that I have loved you...

The lovely Destiny,

Beautiful, smart, and talented can only describe the make-up of you. When you think of genetics, you only began to be comfortable. But when you think of the things most important in life, I can only ask forgiveness. I have not provided the stability in your life that would give you the leverage to succeed. And yet, you are at the top in everything you do. Destiny, love and support and security are my responsibility as your father. It was not my goal to fail at making sure these necessities were a part of your youth. You deserve to come into this world with the best that could be provided to you. Trying is not enough. Where you live and the friendships that you acquire are important to feeling secure and well-rounded. Please forgive me for not providing the things that would have given you friendships that would have endured a lifetime. With great hope, you've known my love....

You'll Never Be Nothing

One son Gianni Dipaolo,

God's greatest gift, a son. Gianni, you were my salvation. My only saving grace in that I could unwrite all the injustice I felt was done to me. But I must also ask your forgiveness. When you were born, I was so afraid of the life that I was currently providing. I was afraid the opportunity to be a great father would be overshadowed by my failures. My inability to protect you and provide you with a home and a secure surrounding was compounded by my emotional fears. You are so intelligent and so capable in all that you do. You are a wild child to look upon you, but you score far beyond all who come in to contact with you. I can only hope that you have known and felt my love for you. As you mature into manhood, always be there for your sisters as you have been there for them as their younger brother...

Sasha the wonder child,

It's so hard to believe you came into this world three months early and at only 2 lbs. I was afraid to touch you. You were the size of one of my hands and perfect. Little face and eyes. You were always so special to me, as I came to the hospital every night at about eleven-clock to sing to you. You were my first audience, someone to practice on. You are only seven years old and yet, you have lived in eight different residences. Sasha, it was never my intention not to provide you with a home and a life that was protected and secure. To hear you pray to God, giving thanks for the meals we eat, is precious. I am sure God is truly moved at what you pray. Please forgive me for not providing you with the security you deserve. As your father, I feel it is important to give you love and a home where you can have friendships. Please know with all my heart that I have loved you...

Author Biography

D'everett-White's childhood was marred by an abusive alcoholic father. Helpless against her husband's unsavory behavior, his loving mother did whatever she could to help her son survive, she was never aware of the abuse, but made sure her son made it to every audition, rehearsal and performance. After years of mental, physical, and sexual abuse, 'White is an accomplished Ballet, Jazz and Tap-dancing performer and choreographer with experience spanning his entire lifetime Donn eventually found his way out through the performing arts. Later he had the opportunity to add acting to his repertoire, and he found himself drawn to performing before live audiences – the bigger the better! Despite being an abuse victim plagued by self-doubt, he was able to overcome some of the identity and intimacy issues once he stood center stage...By the time he met and married his wife, Domino. Coming from a very loving family, she was not prepared for the ongoing struggles Donn experienced as the residual effects of the abuse. However, they worked through the difficulties, and remained married for twenty years. They are the proud parents of four children, three girls and one boy. In some ways, this is a Hollywood story-not because it has a happy "Hollywood" ending, but because this memoir's author grew up in the entertainment industry and found there both the demons that threatened to derail him and the saving grace that continually drove him to perform before audiences and to find his way again.

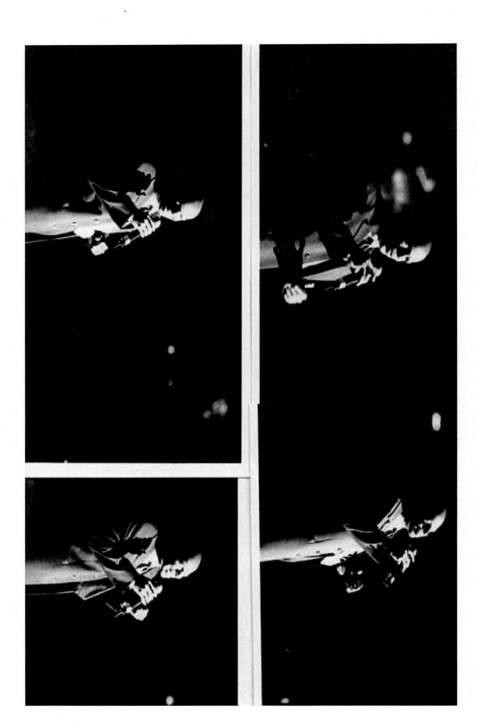